Gweimui's

Hong Kong

Wet Markets

Christine Cappio

The Commercial Press

To my Mum, Lucien

and Yan

Gweimui's Hong Kong Wet Markets

Written by:	Christine Cappio
Edited by:	Betty Wong
Cover designed by:	Cathy Chiu
Illustrations by:	Christine Cappio
Published by:	The Commercial Press (H.K) Ltd.,
	8/F, Eastern Central Plaza, 3 Yiu Hing Road,
	Shau Kei Wan, Hong Kong
	http://www.commercialpress.com.hk
Distributed by:	The SUP Publishing Logistics (H.K.) Ltd.,
	3/F, C & C Building, 36 Ting Lai Road,
	Tai Po, New Territories, Hong Kong
Printed by:	C & C Offset Printing Co. Ltd.,
	14/F, C & C Building, 36 Ting Lai Road,
	Tai Po, New Territories, Hong Kong

© 2019 The Commercial Press (H.K.) Ltd.
First Edition, July 2019

ISBN 978 96207 0564 9

Printed in Hong Kong

Contents

Part 13: Gardening 249

Part 14: English-Cantonese Vocabulary of shopping at wet markets 259

Part 15: *Illustrations of some popular local vegetables and spices*

Conclusion

Acknowledgements

Foreword I

This book honors what no Hongkonger would neglect: the appetite for fine cuisine.

With subtlety and humor, Christine Cappio offers a glimpse into the intimacy of the city's food markets. Her drawings describe the unique atmosphere of each location. More than a guide, she offers us a perspective. Coming from France, a country which attaches great importance to its gastronomy, she decides to take a leap forward and sweep away her prejudices, with the ambition of becoming a true Hong Kong cook!

Gastronomy is an ancestral art and a key feature of all great civilizations. China and France share this. As Lin Yutang (1895-1976), a famous Fujian scholar influenced by Western culture, put it in 1937, "every meal on each day is a Feast of Life". Aren't most of the "Thirty-Three Happy Moments" described by Jin Shengtan (1608-1661), Suzhou's "Prince of Commentators", related to the pleasure of eating? To achieve this, the Chinese have chopsticks, the French have their "coup de fourchette" (literally fork's blow) which means they are big eaters.

Wet markets are at the core of this common culture. Food needs to be looked at, touched and smelled before being sliced, simmered, fried or steamed, and eventually landed on our plates! There is magic in this whole process. This is why great chefs are, whether in Paris or in Hong Kong, surrounded by an aura of mystery. But there is one ingredient you cannot do without: freshness. She is the mother of all flavors. It is so true that the three words "fish", "fresh" and "tasty" share the same character in classical Chinese: xian（鮮）.

In an era where everything tends to be sanitized, wet markets remind us that a city is an organism that has a soul, a heartbeat and also a belly. *The Belly of Paris* was the title that French writer Emile Zola chose in 1873 for his novel describing the life in Les Halles, the city's central market. Our markets are living organs that retain their picturesque character and remain meeting places where colours, smells and noises interact. In Hong Kong, where space is scarce and disputed, markets are faced with the challenge of being replaced by the development projects of business or shopping centres. In this respect, Christine Cappio's strolling in the wet markets is also a manifesto: let us fight to be able to experience this maze of alleys and backstreets, smells and flavors, with our grandchildren when tomorrow comes!

The banquet of life is right in front of us, and the only question is how much appetite we have for it!

Alexandre Giorgini
Consul General of France in Hong Kong and Macao

Foreword II

I am doubly privileged to be invited to write the preface for Ms Christine Cappio's second book. This time it is about another fascinating Hong Kong institution – the wet market.

As a cosmopolitan city where East meets West, Hong Kong has no shortage of modern and large-scale supermarkets. Many, however, still prefer to go to wet markets to source their groceries and fresh food, which is the essence of Cantonese cuisine and a distinct feature of Hong Kong's social landscape.

The traditional wet market is another symbol of Hong Kong culture with its special ambience and vendors typifying the Hong Kong spirit of self-reliance, vibrancy and diversity. Open daily, wet markets around Hong Kong offer a rich array of fresh groceries, from meat, sea food, to vegetables, fruits and bean curd, at a reasonable price, within convenient distance and with a warm human touch.

When Christine arrived in Hong Kong from her native France decades ago, her mother-in-law is a local Chinese who had warned her to stay away from wet markets because they were "smelly, dirty and slippery". But that did not stop her from exploring these bustling and colourful bazaars and finding their enduring charm. In the process, she gathered insights to offer us a complete picture of the wet market, from how to buy stuff to tricks of the trade, and show the reader how to enjoy the experience.

These days, not many local residents go to wet markets. They prefer to shop in the comfort of supermarkets and convenience stores. Indeed, it is rare to find an expatriate lady in a wet market. So I highly commend the adventurous and inquisitive spirit that led Christine to immerse herself in an interesting feature of Hong Kong's unique and traditional culture to bring us another delightful little book. This publication vividly reflects Christine's strong affection for Hong Kong and passion for Chinese culture.

Matthew Cheung Kin-chung
Chief Secretary for Administration
The Government of the Hong Kong Special Administrative Region

Foreword III

When Christine finished her first book, *Gweimui's Hong Kong Story*, I had the privilege to have a preview. I told her that I learnt a few things from her manuscript, not because she knew what I didn't know of about Hong Kong but her writings gave me a new perspective to look at what I'm familiar with. Her observations alert me to angles that I am not fully aware of. As a sociologist, I know very well about how unfamiliarity would help me understand and unravel the deeper meanings of the so-called familiar. Her fresh and observant eyes guide me to understand Hong Kong in a new light.

In this second book of Christine's (and I bet this will be the second title of the *Gweimui* series and I expect more to follow), she looks at Hong Kong's wet market. She knows a lot about it and, I must say, a lot more than I do. I must confess that when I was young I hated our local wet markets (and whether they are open-air or multi-storey indoor is just the same to me). They are smelly, wet, muddy, slippery, noisy, and dirty. As a kid growing up in a public housing estate, I was often assigned to do some shopping for our family. It was an assignment; I was told when to go and what to do. I only needed to cross one road, with the assistance of traffic light, to reach the market along Marble Road and this was supposed to be reasonably safe and easily do-able (according to the expectations in the 1960s, we could handle this household task once we reached the age of nine or ten). Grandmother and / or mother would give me the instructions and then handed me the money. The incentive was that I could use 10 or 20 cents out of that amount to buy my favourite snacks.

Frankly, I always had difficulties in approaching the stalls that sold poultry; I hated the smell of the fish table; and I did not quite follow the butchers' "dress code". But gradually I got used to it and when I grew up I began to see the richness of social life in our wet markets. The feeling is similar to how I came to appreciate bitter melons: you hated them when you were young, and then later you will change your opinion. Gradually, you'll find most tasty when you grow older. The same for my encounter of wet market.

Again, Christine offers her grounded observations of social life in Hong Kong. The choice of the topic itself will tell you how close she has got to ordinary people's daily life in this city. As expected, she has an interesting (*Gweimui*) story to tell. Meanwhile I began to think: when will she start working on the third title?

Lui Tai-lok
Vice President (Research & Development)
The Education University of Hong Kong

Foreword IV

Paris was where I first met Christine in 1983. The Chinese dim sum restaurant called "Hong Kong" in the 6th district was where we had our first date. A not so romantic first date in a very romantic city! It was Christine's first time trying dim sum. Since then, we went there regularly. I did not cook much in Paris and ate all the time in student canteens, which served western food. I was not picky on food, but barbecue pork bun and shrimp dumplings were a big treat for a Chinese student who studied abroad in Paris. This Chinese restaurant was just like medicine for my homesickness and always reminded me of my hometown – Hong Kong. Christine had no problem eating Chinese food. I still remember I bought a can of snake soup in Chinatown for dinner in the dormitory. She ate it with some hesitation and told me that she felt as if a snake was crawling down her throat.

Christine has been living in Hong Kong since 1986. During her early days here, seeing all the Asian vegetables that could not be found in Europe and the way how we cooked really amazed her. She was curious about Chinese cuisine and asked me many times why my mom put the green and red carrots in the soup but not the green and white carrots. She also found the thousand-year-old egg astonishing – particularly the pungent aroma and black-greyish colour when she opened the egg. When we moved away from my mom's place, we began our own adventures in the wet markets. Both of us had to work and we took turns to do the shopping, sometimes in the wet markets and sometimes in the supermarkets. We have lived in many different districts and got to know different wet markets. At the very beginning, we looked and acted like inexperienced customers, thus always suspecting that we might have been cheated. Now we are no longer novices, but regular customers who will be offered additional spring onions or a few dollars' discount from time to time. We shop at least once a week together in the Tai Po wet market.

My experience about French markets started when we returned to Lyon after our marriage. Going to the market in Vienne on every Saturday morning is a big event for Christine's family. It is indeed a wonderful experience in the summer time. The stalls are set up on the streets and the whole area is turned into a pedestrian district. Every Saturday morning, one can virtually find everybody there. People spend the whole morning there shopping and chatting with each other. You stop every 5 minutes to greet someone you know. People talk about politics, weather, family or gardening. Usually you will end up in the local cafe for a drink. During my first visit to Christine's family, the Saturday market of Vienne was where I met her family friends and neighbours for the first time. They were curious to see me in real – Christine's Chinese husband. I guess the whole village had been gossiping about Christine's family and wondering why Christine had chosen a Chinese as her husband because inter-racial marriages were not common at that time, particularly in a small French village.

I have always enjoyed the more relaxed atmosphere of French street markets. I feel that the Hong Kong markets always give you a rushed feeling as people are at all times in a hurry to do their shopping. Whenever we return to France, we would still go to enjoy the Saturday market in Vienne. But now nobody is curious in seeing me with Christine's family anymore. I have also become accustomed to the pace of French everyday life and take my time to shop and chat with people in the market.

Over the past 30 plus years, Christine has transformed from a Gweimui who could not speak a word of Cantonese to a Gweipo who can communicate and sometimes even bargain with the stall sellers in fluent Cantonese. I am so glad that now I need not be bombarded with loads of questions about Chinese food anymore.

Stephen Cheung Yan-leung
President
The Education University of Hong Kong

Introduction

I love green markets and I have always loved them. My interest started when I was about 10 years old and big enough to accompany my mum on her market errands at the nearby town.

There was no market in the village where I grew up and the closest one was about 2 km from where we lived. It took us about half an hour to walk there and a bit longer to come back since we had to carry full bags of produce, meats and cheese, etc. The outdoor market took place once a week and I could only go during school breaks as we had school on Saturday mornings. My parents did their monthly grocery shopping at a hypermarket near Lyon and seldom brought their three children (my sister, brother and me), as we were easily tempted by sweets and other unnecessary things and more importantly we could have got lost in the long crowded aisles. Therefore, going to the market was a very exciting outing for me. I can still recall my joy at this fun event. Not only that I was helping my mum to carry back her shopping bags full of fresh food for the week ahead, but I could meet some of my classmates and taste cheese at the cheesemonger. And when there were sales, I could also get new clothes.

Since then marketplaces made a deep impression on me, and getting close to vendors as well as meeting people have always attracted me. Every time I return to my hometown, I never miss this weekly event and I still find it as much fun today as it was when I was a child.

I was so thrilled to discover the markets in Hong Kong when I came to live in this city back in 1986. They were in many ways different from those in France. The butchers' stalls smelled stale blood and meat and the ground near the veggies and fish stalls was slippery, hence the name "wet" markets. I felt quite at a loss surrounded by so many foods I had never seen before, most of them without price or nametags.

However, I liked the lively atmosphere of Hong Kong wet markets and these drawbacks did not discourage me from exploring them. Learning how to buy at the market had been an exciting journey.

Talking about green markets led me to speak about food, French cuisine and my upbringing in a traditional French family. Food is a wide topic and I am always amazed by the passion with which people talk about what they eat and their willingness to give you advice on how to cook this and that. Food is not only a basic need to our physical life but is also of great importance to each nation's culture, particularly at festivals. Eating is a pleasure. It is said that French live to eat when most people eat to live, and the saying is true with Hong Kong people. Food is life and health.

Finally, I would like to encourage everyone and each one of my readers, be they locals or non-locals, to venture and explore these lively and cultural places and learn to appreciate their atmosphere and benefits. Be adventurous, try new ingredients and produce, don't be shy and ask stallholders to share with you their recipes and experiment!

Hong Kong wet markets are fun places to walk around and buy!

Christine Cappio

Note: As for my previous and 1st book, "Gweimui's Hong Kong Story" published in 2016, I will offer the royalties from this book to charitable organisations.

Part 1

First experience at
Hong Kong markets

Warning: "Don't go to the wet market!"

I first came to Hong Kong during the summer of 1985 for my summer holiday. The aim of my visit was to meet my boyfriend's family and see with my own eyes the city where he was born. I also wanted to see if I would like to live there. Although I could only explore a tiny part of this wonderful place during my short one-month stay, I already fell in love with its food, culture and inhabitants. I stayed with my boyfriend's family in Wanchai district, and would always give a furtive look at the wet market on a few occasions when we were passing through Wanchai Road on our way to Queen's Road East, to take the cross-harbour tunnel bus to visit his grand-parents in Tai Po or his alma mater, The Chinese University of Hong Kong, in Shatin. I was then on holiday and did not need to buy anything at the market as my future mother-in-law cooked for us. I just looked bewilderingly at the many strange things displayed along the streets.

Ten months later, I came back to Hong Kong to join my boyfriend. Little did I know that I would get married less than one month later and built my life in this city that I today call home. Before moving to our own home, we lived for 6 months with my mother-in-law, who worked in a pharmaceutical factory in Aberdeen. Like most Chinese people, she did not like to keep meat and veggies in the fridge, as she believed they were no longer fresh nor nutritious. That is why she insisted on visiting the market every evening after her long day at work and bought fresh food for the family dinner. My mother-in-law used to do her shopping on Wanchai Road which was a 5-minute walk from where she lived. I never had the opportunity to accompany her as she went there straight after work. She knew I would have liked to go with her, but said I needn't have to. She thought the market was too smelly, dirty and slippery. Besides, although she did not say it, I knew I would have caused her trouble. Firstly, Mammy, as I called her, did not speak English and I could not yet speak Cantonese so we could not communicate with each other apart from smiling and making funny gestures. Secondly, I would have slowed her down as I would have looked around and stared in amazement at the various gourds that were new to me. Thirdly, she would have been afraid of losing me in this throng of people and would have needed to hold my hand as if I were a little girl, which might have embarrassed me a bit. And what if I had injured myself slipping and falling on the wet floor at the fishmongers'?

After considering all the above points, I did not insist. Had I listened to all these negative comments, I would have stayed away from the markets. But I had to satisfy my curiosity and thus started exploring Wanchai Road on my own!

紀詩婷, wet markets are smelly, dirty and slippery. Don't go!

Mammy said I need not go to the market,

because wet markets were smelly,

dirty,

and slippery.

Observing

I wanted to know what the strange-looking ochre bean curd sticks, the gluten balls, the bat-shaped seed pods and those sauces packed in small plastic bags hung on wire racks were. I was curious and wanted to taste them all at once. I asked my husband so many questions: "What are those pale yellow sticks and sheets?" (dried tofu skin), "What are these little ochre balls?" (deep-fried bean curd), "How to cook this?", "Is that good?" and so on. However, at times he himself could not furnish all the answers I expected.

The wet markets in Hong Kong were indeed quite different in some ways from those in France. But all the same I loved the atmosphere, the flow of people and the colourful presentations. The goods and smells were not the same. I missed the aroma of roasted chicken drifting through the air at the French markets. Although I had sold tripe at two street markets when I was a student to pay for my trip to Hong Kong and had seen plenty of fresh meat at that time, I had never seen meat displayed as it was in Hong Kong.

During my first months in Hong Kong, I enjoyed looking at people buying at the market, the interactions between customers and sellers and the many products that were new to me. There were lots of strange stuff such as green gourds with blistered skin (bitter melon), brown tubulars (lotus roots and kudzu), woody ugly-looking rhizome (Chinese yam) and long thin hairy roots looking like salsify (burdock). The most beautiful food was certainly the dragon fruit with its soft and thick pink skin and scales turning green at their tips. The carrots were so big that I thought they were meant for cows' consumption. I also discovered other big roots, some were green (Oriental radish) and other white (turnips).

I was flabbergasted to see shops extending their business areas onto the pavements and hawkers lining up the road as well as the enormous quantity of food amassed in a small place. Hong Kong stallholders were smart and made use of every nook and cranny due to the limited place and high rent. Goods were everywhere, hung on metal grilles and bars or massed on shelves and tables. The maximizing of the space utilisation was really amazing. Despite the limited amount of space in the stalls, sellers provided their customers with as many choices as possible and were very efficient. For instance, imported and local baby or plantain bananas were hung on metal bars above the stalls, allowing air to circulate and slow down the ripening. This could also save some space. In France, each bunch of bananas was in a plastic basin as the weather was not as hot as in Hong Kong. Veggies and fruit were stacked high.

I loved the verticality and visual effect of the displays and I admired the beautiful piles of morning glory (water spinach). The pattern formed by the tips of the hollow and thick stems was really beautiful. Similarly, in France I liked to see the way the white asparagus were displayed in May when they were in season, standing upright looking like bundles of twigs. But comparatively displays were rather flat in France. Given that the turnover was not as high as in Hong Kong, stallholders did not have to overload their tables and preferred to display their goods gradually. The other things that caught my eyes were the metal hooks at the butcher's and grocers', the buckets attached to a string serving as money-bags, the ceiling fans and the red lights that are one of Hong Kong's icons. Yes, the market place was dotted with red lampshades diffusing a red halo on greens, fruit, meat and fish, and making them look fresher. Even during daytime and in the hottest days of the year, all commodities were in the spotlight!

On Wanchai Road as double-parked delivery vans were obstructing the traffic flow, shoppers would wriggle through the congested area in the sweltering heat. Further up in the Bauhaus-style building located at the corner of Queen's Road East was an indoor market in which I never ventured. I can't recall exactly why and I regret it, but I guess the confined and smelly environment must have put me off and frightened me. This was how I discovered why markets in Hong Kong were called wet markets rather than farmer's markets. The logic was that greens, fish and meat were "wet" in comparison with "dry" items like clothes, accessories, toys or kitchenware. Furthermore, stalls selling fresh produce were literally wet. As Mammy had warned me, the floor was slippery with water overflowing from fish tanks and greens that were sprayed with water by sellers in order to make them stay fresh and attractive as long as possible, as well as the occasional bits of fat discarded by butchers. Shoppers had better watch their steps.

I was so curious about everything that I bombarded my husband with questions.

I saw lots of strange stuff, such as green gourds with blistered skin (bitter melon) and carrots so big that I thought they were meant for cows' consumption.

I had never seen meat displayed like this.

Hiding

Later my husband and I moved to Chi Fu Fa Yuen in Pokfulam area to live on our own and there we did our own shopping. We bought food at the market in the shopping centre of the residential complex. Unlike the market on Wanchai Road, the floor was clean and dry and the place was air-conditioned. In the weekend, we went shopping in Pokfulam village. There were fewer stalls and fewer options there, but the place was more original and food was cheaper. On the steps of their tin-roofed houses, villagers sold small quantity of veggies right on the ground or in wicker baskets. I remember an elderly woman who sold homemade bean curd pudding in a large wooden bucket; she scooped the white jelly into small ceramic bowls. This is where I tried the soft bean curd for the first time. At that time, I found it too bland without a spoonful of ginger sugar and syrup.

At first, my husband did not want me to go with him as he thought it was dirty and wanted to spare me this chore. Furthermore, I did not know how to buy Chinese goods and market vendors were known for cheating novice shoppers.

I recall my husband's ruse when we went together for market shopping. Do you know what he did? He asked me to stand at a distance away from him while he was making his purchases. Was he ashamed of his wife being a "Gweimui", the name that locals give familiarly to Caucasian girls? No, he was not. Then, why did he ask me not to stand next to him? He thought it was better if vendors did not know he was married to a "ghost girl", fearing that they would cheat him. Was it a reason for charging him more? Sure, I did not look Chinese and we did not look like experienced shoppers who knew the prices and the sellers' tricks. We were an easy target to get ripped off. Nobody, even the French, likes to be cheated and pay more than what is due. So I resigned myself to my husband's ruse and waited for him in a corner while he did our wet market shopping. But who knows if he has ever been cheated too when he shopped on his own!

My husband's trick – I hid myself while he was making his purchases.

Learning how to buy

I was interested in learning to cook Chinese dishes and hence needed to buy local ingredients. I did not mind the roughness of markets, but had to, firstly, overcome the apprehension that sellers would see me as an ignorant foreigner who could be easily cheated, and secondly, learn to speak Cantonese.

Hong Kong sellers were efficient. They did not bother with unnecessary information and did not write the names of the produce. Locals could recognise the food they wanted to buy and could ask; I could not! I felt particularly lost at the fish sellers' and butchers'. Not only there were no names but very often, there were no prices as well. Besides, even when there were signs, I could not read the red-coloured Chinese numbers and characters written on brown cardboard pricked among heaps of vegetables or Styrofoam on top of fish buckets.

I was able to recognise spare ribs and pork knuckles and could point at them with my fingers, but I did not want to eat only those. I wanted to be able to order meat at wet markets like the locals.

One of the differences in the way people buy meat in Hong Kong is that they ask for the amount of money that they want to buy, for instance, "HK$15 of lean pork" or "HK$20 of minced pork".

I could have asked my husband to write down in Chinese what I wanted, like many families did for their domestic helpers. Then I would just need to show my shopping list to the vendors and thus it would not have been necessary for me to speak. But this would not have been a long-term solution.

Therefore, I asked my husband to teach me the names of cuts and foodstuffs, and recorded them with my own way in Latin alphabet. Slowly I learnt by myself how to recognise the veggies, how to read prices in Chinese, the different units of weights used in Hong Kong: pound, tael or catty, as well as the characters for piece or bunch. I drew up my own list of useful vocabulary.

Buying at the market forced me to speak and listen to Cantonese, as many sellers were not fluent in English, giving non-Chinese speakers, like me, an opportunity to practise. One thing that was amusing was the funny intonation vendors took when they spoke to me, which at first I found rather peculiar and mocking. Later I learnt that they wanted to copy the intonation of foreigners, thinking that we could better understand them this way.

At first, I felt intimidated and did not dare speaking too much. If my intonation was wrong, the sellers simply did not understand me and it disturbed me. I would have liked them to be more imaginative. Could they not make an effort and just try to figure out the words that I said with another tone? However, it did not work this way and they could not guess. I had to learn to be patient and most of all to be persistent in my learning. I learnt to repeat until I was understood.

Doing my grocery shopping at the market helped me overcome the fear of speaking Cantonese, and become more independent and develop a sense of belonging to the local society. However, my learning experience has not been without any disappointments, such as being overcharged, given old veggies or pushed to buy more. Some encounters had been quite interesting such as when I discovered Chinese finger gestures.

My frustration when the sellers did not understand me because of my funny intonation.

My homework – to record the names of foodstuffs in Latin alphabet.

I learnt how to read the signs in Chinese. Bravo!

Weighing issues

At first, I could not tell if the Chinese vegetables were fresh, ripe, old or coarse. People could tell I was a foreigner, I was an easy prey and could be easily cheated.

I recall my first experiences at Pokfulam village market where the sellers were so quick at weighing the goods. Was I paying for the actual weight? I was a Gweimui and had difficulty in evaluating how heavy one Chinese carrot was and how many green leaves were in a catty. I had heard stories that vendors would spray water on the veggies to add weight to them, but I believed it was to keep their produce fresh, which made sense particularly in hot weather. How much water a catty of bok choy can contain and how many more cents can you be cheated of? In order to avoid being cheated too much, I tried to listen to how much the customers around me were asked to pay so that I could figure out the amount I would have to pay. However, I admit that this tactic was very difficult to put into practice and was not always accurate.

Furthermore, in Hong Kong the standard unit of weight

is catty[1], not mentioning the different currency. Back in 1986, 1 FRF was equivalent to about HK$1.2. All these added to my confusion.

Sellers were so swift; in no time at all my batch of bok choy was put on the scale plate and thrown into a plastic bag or wrapped up in newspapers. I was even more confused at the Wanchai Road market where most of the sellers hanged veggies to a hook of a Chinese traditional scale. The beam went up and down so fast that it was impossible to check if the weight was right or not and it seemed that locals never questioned the sellers' skill. It was part of the market experience and clients trusted the sellers whom they patronised. Today it is slightly better with mechanical scales, but it is still difficult to see where the red hand stabilises as it shows two weights, in pound and in catty, and the experienced sellers read fast and remove the items from the bowl very quickly. If you have any doubt, it is possible to check if vendors have given you the right weight with the mechanical scales that the Hong Kong Government has put at the disposal of customers at indoor markets. I see people using them from time to time.

I recall once I bought an old cucumber (yellow cucumber) from a lady seller whom I had never bought from. The lady charged me for one catty. I was wondering how come the gourd could weigh exactly one catty. I then naively supposed that she had perhaps rounded it down and given

---

[1]   A catty = 630 gr. = 16 taels.

me a discount and was thinking whether I should thank her. Anyway, there was no point in asking, but I was not surprised at all to find it weigh much less later when I checked its weight at home! This is not only typical of Hong Kong wet markets; vendors all over the world use the same tricks and it is no use arguing for a few cents. If you are not a regular customer, you will be an easy prey and hopefully, vendors with whom you are familiar with will not trick you!

Another thing you need to be careful is to check the unit price, especially that of vegetables sold in bunches. In Hong Kong, it is common to find long vegetables such as long beans, Chinese flowering cabbage, Chinese water spinach or the longer variety of bok choy, tied up in bundles with a rubber band or red raffia and nicely stacked up. However, do not always assume that each pack weighs one catty especially when other prices nearby are per catty. You might be surprised if you check later at home to find out that your pack of bok choy weighs half of what you thought. Ready-to-buy bunches is a good way to speed up sales and in France it is the greengrocers' common and main practice. Hong Kong stallholders do the same as it makes even more sense here considering the quick flow of customers.

A puzzle to me – how come the gourd could weigh exactly one catty?

I found it weighed much less when I checked its weight at home!

Sellers' tricks

Have you ever been pushed to buy more than you ask for? It happens quite often and it becomes more obvious when the goods are more expensive (for example, dried seafood). I am used to buying walnuts for my homemade bread at a market stall. The price by pound is clearly written on a bright orange paper and I always ask for one pound at a time, but very often end up buying more than I plan to. The seller fills up the bag with walnuts and after a quick look at the scale, she announces in a low voice a price which is far higher than the price for one pound. The first time I told her that it was too much and did not want to store so much at home, and asked her to remove some. Then I said to myself, "why bother? At the end of the day I will make use of the nuts." I call it "positive cheating" as the extra money that I do not intend to spend in the first place is for my benefit.

The seller always puts more than I need
– a tactic to sell more!

Old produce

For many years, I stuck to the usual choices, namely bok choy, Chinese kale and Chinese flowering cabbage. Later, once I became more fluent in Cantonese I started to look around for vegetables that I had never tried and would ask the vendors how to cook them.

However, I recall that at times when I bought from stalls I had never patronised before and vendors realised I knew nothing, I encountered a few misfortunes. This had been the case when I bought kudzu. The vendor was kind enough to teach me how to make a soup with it by adding to the ugly-looking root adzuki beans, pork bones and fish. He also praised the virtue of kudzu, claiming that it could eliminate body dampness, but he did not warn me that the root was old – therefore quite fibrous and too tough to eat. Another time I bought arrowhead tubers somewhere else. I should have observed that the flesh was soft and the roots were not fresh. Thereafter I never returned to these stalls and from then on spent more time to check if goods were fresh or not before buying.

This way of cheating people with old vegetables makes me recall a bad joke about British youths who came to visit their French penfriends in the 1950s and had never had artichokes before. The French students did not tell them that the centre of the bulb and the upper portion of the leaves of the artichoke were not edible. You can easily imagine the poor students biting into the hard parts before their peers stopped them! In my case and unlike the students, the seller was not there to watch me biting into the fibrous or mushy roots. The artichoke is not popular in Hong Kong and not many people know how to eat it. Restaurants only use the heart of the vegetable, which is soft, and we can't see how the whole plant looks like.

The vendor was kind enough to teach me how to make a soup with kudzu,

claiming that it could eliminate body dampness,

but he forgot to warn me that the root was old and too tough to eat.

Chinese finger gestures

I recall one funny story when I was not yet aware of how Chinese people used their fingers to indicate the numbers from one to ten. This happened at the butcher's in Chi Fu Fa Yuen. The butcher had prepared the meat and when giving it to me, he asked me in Cantonese to pay: "sap[6]-luk[6] man[1]" (HK$16) which literally means 10+6-dollars. However, I heard wrongly and thought it was HK$15 (10+5-dollars) and thus gave him a HK$10 green bill and a HK$5 coin. He did not take the money, but looked at me repeating "sap[6]-luk[6] man[1]" while at the same time pointing his thumb and little finger downward. Seeing two fingers, I thought he was asking for HK$12 (which is 10+2-dollars) and promptly took out a wavy-edged coin embossed with the Queen Elizabeth II head out of my wallet. The butcher started to show his impatience and showed again his hand with his extended thumb and little finger and his three middle fingers closed. I was confused. For me, two fingers meant 2. The situation started to get embarrassing as more customers were queuing up, waiting for the Gweimui to hurry and pay so that they could be finally served. Suddenly a client got me out of this dilemma shouting in English "16 dollars!" I then realised I had not been listening carefully, but just looking at his hand. Without wasting more time, I looked into my purse and hurried to settle my purchase. I left the place reflecting on what I had just learnt: Chinese people use two fingers to represent number six.

The butcher asked me in Cantonese to pay: "sap⁶ luk⁶ man¹".

I misunderstood it as HK$15 and gave a $10 bill plus a $5 coin.

The butcher kept repeating in Cantonese "sap⁶ luk⁶ man¹" and pointed two fingers. I thought he was asking for HK$12 and so replaced my $5 coin by a $2 coin. Finally a client got me out of this dilemma by shouting in English "16 dollars!"

I then realised that pointing two fingers is the Chinese finger gesture for number six.

Experimenting new produce

Later I started exploring different markets in Mongkok and Tai Po and bought vegetables that were less common: wild rice shoots, stem lettuce, Chinese box thorn, mustard cabbage, cow horn peppers, etc.

I recall when I bought dracontomelon, a little fruit that is nicknamed man-in-the-moon fruit and used to make a peculiar sauce which combines stem ginger, minced pork and yellow bean paste. I thought I would try to make some. However, the result was disappointing. My husband did not comment and had only a spoonful. I knew what this meant. I liked the crunchy flesh and spicy taste of the stem ginger, but it was overpowering and I could not really taste the dracontomelon flavour. I had certainly put too much ginger. The friend who had given me the recipe had told me that the flesh around the seed was delicious and its lemony aftertaste was refreshing after biting on ginger shreds. It would have been a pity not to keep it, and I ate it all with a bowl of steamed rice and rice shoots that I had stir-fried on that day. My sauce for sure gave a boost to their rather bland taste! After my unsuccessful experience, I thought I'd better buy the commercial paste which is available at traditional grocers during a short period of time when stem ginger is in season from May to July, and try to eat it in a lettuce wrap. As of today, I have not done it yet. The only souvenirs of my defeat are the white seeds that I kept and displayed on my desk. I like the markings on them that look like aliens' eyes, like ET's in the famous Sci-fi movie.

I bought dracontomelon, a little fruit that is nicknamed "man-in-the-moon fruit", and made a sauce with it and ...

my husband had only one spoonful and did not comment.
OK, I knew what this meant.

Part 2

Markets in France

Temporary and permanent markets

The concept of the marketplace dates back to the Middle Ages when farmers started to bring their produce to the nearest city to sell. The oldest covered retail market in Paris, the Marché des Enfants Rouges located in the Marais district, dates back to the 17th century. And, Paris' Les Halles, a centralised covered wholesale market depicted as the "Belly of Paris" in Zola's eponymous novel, was built in the early 12th century.

France has a long history of markets with more than 10,000 traditional markets all over the country. Traditional producers are in higher numbers and only a handful of stands sell organic vegetables.

Most of them are temporary and held on a weekly basis from very early in the morning until lunchtime. They are held outdoors, usually on large streets with wide sidewalks, city plazas, in front of the churches or city halls, or even on parking lots. Some are held in "halles" (market buildings). Some covered markets are paired with an outdoor market and are held once a week.

The permanent markets are either held outdoors, like the famous Rue Mouffetard and Rue Montorgueil markets in Paris, or indoors. Some indoor markets accommodate chic restaurants and are open the whole day from Tuesday to Sunday noon. Per French regulations, they are closed on Sunday afternoons and Mondays. Les "Halles Paul Bocuse" is one of them. The covered market, named after the famous Lyonnais chef, is the largest covered market in Lyon and opened in 1859. It has a few gourmet shops as well as famous cheesemongers and sellers of cured and cooked meats (charcuterie), some of them offering ready-cooked dishes for customers to enjoy on their terrace.

French markets are not limited to food and you can also find flowers, clothes, accessories, etc., but the main attractions are the local produce sold by farmers. Greengrocers who don't grow the produce they sell are also present, but the smaller the city the fewer stalls you will find. Therefore, the chance to find bananas or any exotic fruit at a small town market is very unlikely.

French rotisserie is a feature of French outdoor markets and can be compared to Chinese roasted meat shops. Who will not succumb to the smell of a delicious roasted chicken and knuckles rotating on pits? Furthermore, who has time to prepare lunch after a morning of shopping? It is so convenient to buy one or half a bird accompanied with roasted potatoes for one's lunch.

At the biggest markets, there are usually one or two stalls dedicated to fresh mushrooms. French are fond of fresh shiitake, and can buy the South-East-Asia native fungus (produced in France) as well as cultured button mushrooms, that French call Paris mushrooms, all year round. Furthermore, in autumn seasonal vendors come to sell wild chanterelles and death trumpets, and some come as far as the south-west of France to sell their truffles.

Some people prefer to go mushroom hunting in forests rather than to buy the fungus already picked. It is a great pleasure to look for the scented fungus hidden under the brown autumn leaves and be able to pick enough to make one's lunch. I recall when I went with my parents to pick horns of plenty (or black chanterelles) in autumn. My parents would only pick the species that they were certain to be edible and could recognise easily. Whenever they feared the mushrooms could be poisonous, they brought them to the nearest pharmacy where they asked for an expert's advice. Picking mushrooms was a great outdoor outing. We also brought sandwiches and drinks, with a thermos of coffee, and enjoyed our picnic in a clearing. Food and rest were most welcome especially when we were empty-handed or our collect did not match our appetite. When the harvest was good and our baskets were full, my mum would stir-fry part of it and put the rest outdoors in the sunlight. After a few days, the dried fungus would be stored and kept for a winter stew or an accompaniment to a roast.

In autumn, I went with my parents to pick up mushrooms.

We enjoyed our picnic in a clearing, savouring the sandwiches and drinks that we brought with a thermos of coffee.

This is poisonous!

Whenever my parents suspected that some of the mushrooms could be poisonous, they brought them to the nearest pharmacy for expert advice.

Some mushrooms sellers also sell freshly picked acacia and elder flowers to make doughnuts with. The blossoms of the edible kind elderberry trees are used to make fritters with.

Farmers who keep bees sell honey infused with flavours depending on the season and types of flowers and plants from which bees have gathered pollen and nectar. Acacia blossoms make a light-coloured honey with a mild flavour and chestnut tree flowers an amber-coloured honey with a stronger taste.

But my favourite stalls are those of the cheesemongers' simply because I can sample their goods. There are so many varieties and sellers are always happy to give you a little bit to try. France has over 350 distinct types of cheese, but each family has its own preferences. Even though we had tried many different kinds, my mum would always buy Comté, Condrieu Rigotte and Auvergne blue cheese plus a new type each week: Savoy Tomme, Saint-Nectaire, Saint-Paulin, etc. We paid no attention

Cheesemongers' were my favourite stalls, simply because I could sample their goods.

to processed cheese as we considered it artificial and tasteless. However, occasionally I would enjoy the wedge-shaped cream cheese, being made famous with a picture of a laughing cow on its wrapping, at the school canteen.

I particularly like the richness and diversity of the Saturday market in Vienne, the town close to where I grew up. France has many other beautiful markets: some are big and some are small, some are famous and some are unheard of. One has even been qualified as the winner of a national competition held in 2018, and some are only held during the Christmas season.

Vienne's Saturday market

In Vienne, located 30 km south of Lyon, the Saturday market is the second biggest outdoor traditional market in the south-east of France after Nîmes[2] with about 400 stalls spread along the main arteries of the city centre. Although there is no record to tell us when the weekly market was first established, it certainly dates back to the Middle Ages or before as Vienne, located near the Rhone river, was one of the major trading cities of the Roman empire.

Vienne is a historical city and you can visit part of this former Roman provincial capital while shopping. It is particularly enjoyable on Saturday mornings as part of Vienne city centre becomes pedestrian and people can walk freely in the middle of the streets. We'd better be careful when selecting and touching fruit, trying to differentiate the flavour of a 6-month old from a 24-month old Comté or watching the butcher wrapping up chicken legs in a sheet of white butcher paper, because the statue

---

[2] Nîmes is about 200 km from Vienne.

of Virgin Mary might be observing us from Mount Pipet towering the city.

The greengrocers and market farmers' stalls are in the town centre and circle around the community hall on Miremont Plaza. Clothes and accessories stalls are spread along a pedestrian promenade shaded with plane trees as well as in the street leading to Saint Peter Church Plaza. The edifice, which was built, at the end of the 5th century today accommodates a museum that displays ancient mosaics, sculptures, sarcophagi, Roman amphorae, etc. In this part of the town, most of the stalls are specialised in North-African and Turkish goods. This is the place to go if you want to buy fresh mint or halal meat. The usually quiet parking area on weekdays is hardly recognisable on Saturday mornings. A large population of North-African and Turkish descents live in Vienne; the mix of native language and colourful dress gives the place a foreign and lively feel. Caterers are making North-African snacks and hot dishes for take-away. Many people stand by the booth and eat the specialties straight away.

When you are done with your shopping, you can sit down at one of the cafe terraces to admire the timber framing of the unique medieval houses in town or the Roman columns of the Temple of Auguste and Livie (built near the end of the 1st century), or you can simply concentrate on people-watching, one of the great pastimes of Frenchmen!

As early as 4:00 am, greengrocers, market gardeners, fishmongers, butchers, caterers and cheese sellers start unpacking and presenting their goods with great care and skill to attract customers. Each one of them hopes that there will be nothing left to bring back home after the business hours. Sellers have to leave at 1:30 pm the latest because the streets need to be cleared of any rubbish and washed before they reopen to vehicles at 2:00 pm.

Going to the market is a tradition and I will not miss the chance of going to the market whenever I go back to my hometown. People shop in a leisurely way because it is held in the weekend when most French do not work: it is a way to end up the week. For the residents of Vienne and its vicinity, the Saturday market is an important event of the week. It is not only where you can shop, but also where you socialise, gossip and share the latest news. The weekly event is eagerly awaited by both sellers and buyers. You will very likely see someone whom you know and it is quite common to bump into old friends, former classmates and relatives. My mum knows she will meet her neighbours and other regular market-goers on her way to the market. Elderlies are the first ones to do their shopping and the first ones to leave the market. You can see them at the bakers', bread being the last item on their shopping list, when younger people just start their shopping.

Groups form and chat in front of the stalls obstructing the passage. Going from one end of the street to the other end might take you 15 minutes on that day when it would normally take 5 minutes. Vienne, which is not populous at usual time, becomes lively on Saturday mornings,

The statue of Virgin Mary observing us from Mount Pipet.

One of the great pastimes of Frenchmen – to sit down after shopping at the cafe terraces to admire the Roman columns of the Temple of Auguste and Livie or concentrate on people – watching!

The market is not only where you can shop, but also a place where you socialise.

A Saturday market special – to fill up a cup or your own plastic bottle with unpasteurised milk from the huge refrigerated milk tank.

When I was small, fresh cow milk was delivered to our home every day by a farmer who lived on the upper part of our village.

Making my own butter fo fun! After a few days wh considered that the qua would be sufficient to make one toast, I shook container until butter fo and whey separated in t container.

reminding me of Hong Kong crowded places.

You cannot just say "bonjour" and walk on, as chatting is part of the market experience. Some people choose to continue their conversation in one of the many cafes nearby. The terraces are usually full with people who have finished shopping or who are taking a break and meeting friends over a cup of coffee or an aperitif when lunchtime is getting closer. Some shoppers hold weekly gatherings and you are certain to see the same people if you go to a specific cafe at a specific time.

The main focuses are the vegetables and fruit followed by charcuterie, but some parts of the town are dedicated to manufactured goods such as clothes, toys, accessories, hardware goods, kitchenware and fabrics. You can also find plants and flowers. Market gardeners who grow their own produce account for the largest number of stalls. They come as far as 25 km away to sell seasonal and home-grown products. We differentiate market gardeners from greengrocers. The latter set up their merchandise on trestle tables without any frills, but despite their straightforward booths, they are highly visible with their goods in wooden boxes stacked high behind them and under the tables, as well as the large stock in their vans parked nearby. They are also the noisiest and you can hear them from the other side of the plaza shouting on top of their lungs to attract passers-by. They import from warmer climate countries, mainly Spain and Morocco, bananas, lemons, oranges, watermelons, persimmons, pomegranate, grapefruit, bell-peppers, tomatoes, etc. Some of their produce can grow in France, but the imported ones are cheaper than those locally grown. They often sell in bulk, but we can always ask for a smaller quantity and still get a reduction albeit a small one. Local fruit producers sell apples in winter; pears, peaches, plums and apricots in summer.

The number of caterers has increased during the past years. The French have taken a liking to eating take-away food with their family after their grocery shopping. Ethnic or regional food is cooked in large cauldrons in front of you. The waft of wine and spices remind market-goers of their presence. Ethnic food such as paella (Spanish) or couscous (North-African) is cooked outdoors, attracting customers with their pleasant smell. In winter, sauerkraut (Alsace region near the German border) is also very popular. The most daring ones can buy kidneys in Madeira sauce. Ready-cooked dishes such as quenelles (the Lyonnais pike quenelles are famous), stuffed squids, mixed seafood salads, breaded fish and others are sold at pork butchers' and fishmongers'.

There is also a stall that sells Asian grocery such as soya sauce and rice, as well as deep-fried spring rolls that you can eat while shopping. Next to the Asian food stall is a pet bird stall. When I was young, I would have liked to own one of those colourful budgerigars or yellow little canaries. My parents never yielded to my request; they thought it would be too much of a constraint. We were already quite busy with raising hens, rabbits and sheep. In addition, we had one cat and one dog as pets. You might think I was living in a farm... Not at all. Luckily, one day a friend of my dad gave us a budgie couple, which he did not want to keep and I was delighted. My wish had come true. I took care of the pair for a few months until winter came and the little birds caught cold and died. I had not foreseen such a bad ending, and thereafter I did not own any bird until 1995 when a budgie flew into our flat in North Point! I could not but keep it. We bought a cage and a companion for it. This time I kept it for a much longer period of time.

Cheesemongers are in force in Vienne and some stalls are specialised in one type of cheese: the local Rigotte de Condrieu. The pure goat cheese originates from Condrieu, hence its name, a village located at about 10 km south of Vienne. The handmade small cheese got the Appellation (AOC) in 2009 and is wrapped in packs of 3 or 6 pieces that are available in different stages of maturity. The freshest cylindrical discs are at least 8-day old, have an ivory colour and a solid yet smooth consistency; as the cheese ripens, it hardens, its rind becomes bluish and its specific hazelnut flavour gets stronger.

Other stalls specialise in regional specialties such as "Ravioles du Dauphiné", those tiny raviolis filled with Comté cheese and parsley; or "Pogne de Romans", a brioche flavoured with vanilla sugar, orange flower water, lemon and orange zests. The seller gives out bits of brioche to passers-by to try, like shopkeepers do in Macau to entice tourists to buy beef jerky or almond cookies.

Vienne also counts an olive stall with many types of olives and olive oil as well as pickled vegetables and lemon, anchovy, olive and dried tomato paste. The Mediterranean products are kept in large round baskets lined with plastic film displayed on a Provencal-style oil tablecloth matching their bright yellow canopies, thus giving a Provence's warm sensation.

One of the peculiarities of the Saturday market is the huge refrigerated milk tank from where you can either fill up a cup with unpasteurised milk to drink straightaway or your own plastic bottle to bring home. This self-service is environmental friendly and cheaper than milk sold in cartons at supermarkets.

I recall when I was small, a farmer who lived on the upper part of our village delivered fresh cow milk every day to our home. This man came very early in the morning and did not ring the doorbell for fear of waking us up. He just stopped at the gate and refilled the metal milk can that my mum left empty on the low wall next to our entrance. The milk had to be boiled immediately to last longer. It was very creamy and when I was on holiday, I sometimes made my own butter for fun. I collected tiny amounts of cream that had built up on the sides of the jar and put it in a small airtight plastic ramekin. After a few days when I considered that the quantity would be sufficient to make one toast, I shook the container until butter formed and whey separated in the container. I liked to sprinkle my buttered toasts or "tartine" with salt on top.

I did not pay much attention to the fact that I was drinking raw milk until after the farmer had passed away and my mum started buying pasteurised or UHT milk. It took me some time to like the taste of the supermarket's milk with a white and black cow printed on the packaging.

In autumn, the same dairy farmer sold an old French pear variety which he liked to call 'Good Louise' for fun, instead of its real name 'Louise Good'.

Vienne also holds smaller open markets each day of the week, except on Mondays (inevitable French regulation!), in different areas of the city.

Beautiful markets

France counts many beautiful markets that attract locals and tourists alike. These lively places are an integral part of all cities.

Most people have a special feeling for a particular market; it might be that their parents used to go there and know the sellers well. Others might have discovered a market in a city when they were travelling on holiday and like to go back regularly. Families on their way to their summer destination like to stop at markets to buy groceries to get the best regional products there.

Some markets are even livelier in summer when tourists arrive. The paths of the markets become crammed with people. The colourful summer crops: tomatoes, green, red and yellow bell peppers, peaches and apricots as well as the bright coloured parasols protecting sellers and goods from the sun bring a holiday mood and lively atmosphere to the place.

Some markets are only held during the summer when tourists arrive and urban dwellers return to their home town for the holidays. A few have performers, such as in Châtillon-sur-Chalaronne or in Belfort, where a barrel organ player and an accordion player liven up the place respectively. At markets closer to ports, like in Normandy, Brittany, Aquitaine, Provence-Alpes-Côte d'Azur, the tourists particularly like to buy freshly caught fish and taste raw oysters, bay scallops or a platter of seafood with a glass of white wine right at the market. In the southern part of France, they also go to the market to buy olives, olive oil, nougat and honey, in Normandy the famous Camembert cheese made with farm-house milk (unpasteurised milk), butter, crème fraîche and apples, in Brittany buckwheat pancakes, etc. Each market is proud of its regional homemade products, be they veggies, fruits, charcuterie or cheese.

Cahors market in the Occitania region, for example, is renowned for its black truffles. Sarlat-la-Canéda and Bergerac markets in the Périgord, in the south-western part of France, are famous for their "gras" markets held in winter. My parents used to go there each year to buy duck livers to bring home and make foie gras terrine as well as duck meat and liver pâté. They either selected individual livers, or the whole poultry at a lower price per kilogramme as it was unable to see the size of the liver inside the plucked web-footed birds.

When my parents and I used to go rafting one weekend in May in the Ardèche department[3], our second best and important activity after rafting was shopping at the market, for food and also fun. During long weekends and summer holidays, the market in Vallon-Pont-d'Arc[4] was held on a large parking lot. Traders coming as far as 60 km away sold fresh and regional products such as honey and wine. In August, my parents liked to return to Ardèche, but this time to Barjac to make provision of garlic from the market because the regional produce tasted better and was at a better price than in Vienne. The Ardèche department is also famous for its chestnuts.

French love shopping at markets so much that in 2018 a private French TV channel organised a competition for its audience to vote for their favourite green market. The 25 nominees, each representing one of the 25 regions of France, were presented individually to the audience at the end of the 12:00 noon news report. I was in France when the competition was running and had watched a few reportages. Both sellers and clients displayed great enthusiasm and passion at promoting the particularities and regional foods of their markets. At the end of a 2-month competition, the 1st prize was awarded to Sanary-sur-Mer, in the Var department. The market, located by the fishing port and with a history dating back to the

---

[3] Ardèche department is less than 60 km south of Vienne (located in Isère department).
[4] Vallon Pont d'Arc is about 175 km from of Vienne.

15th century, won the heart of the French spectators with its local catch and produce such as lemons, oranges and olives.

Christmas markets

Christmas markets don't have produce, meat and cheese stalls but regional specialities related to Christmas such as the now universal gingerbread cookies. Food as well as handmade toys and other Christmas paraphernalia are sold in wooden huts nicely decorated with fake snow, garlands and lights.

The Alsace region's markets are famous for their lively guided tours in the beautifully decorated streets. People can also take part in activities, for example learn how to bake traditional Alsatian cakes or attend storytelling sessions. The best time to visit these markets is obviously after sunset so as to enjoy the colourful streets and plazas illuminated with lights, garlands and the unmissable huge Christmas trees. The biggest markets last for the whole month of December and open until late in the evening, some until 10:00 pm. People like to take time to visit the place with their friends and enjoy roasted chestnuts and mulled wine. In Lyon people taste oysters and aligot which is cheese blended with mashed potato, an Auvergne speciality.

Lyon also has a very special Christmas sweet named "papillotes". The chocolate sweets are wrapped with a fringed silver or gold-coloured paper and each one has a piece of paper, similar to the fortune cookies, with a riddle or rebus puzzle. The legend says that it all started at the end of the 18th century in the Terreaux district when an assistant confectioner put love messages inside the sweets to seduce his sweetheart who was working on the floor above. Don't the messages smuggled in food remind you of a similar story in Chinese history, namely the folk tale of mooncakes? During the Ming dynasty, the delicacy enjoyed today during the Mid-Autumn Festival was used by the revolutionaries to send messages to coordinate the Han Chinese revolt on the 15th day of the 8th lunar month. The message was either put inside the pastry or printed on top of the mooncakes as a puzzle. Today you can find "papillotes" throughout France.

The legend says that an assistant confectioner put love messages inside the chocolate sweets to seduce his sweetheart who was working on the floor above.

Part 3

Markets in Hong Kong

Private and public markets

Hong Kong also has a long history of street markets. They are very often located in narrow streets between buildings. Most mobile hawkers who were common at the end of the 1980s have now disappeared and sellers rent kiosks on streets, in markets or shops in government buildings. There are only a few itinerant hawkers left selling fruit on carts like those who sell on trestle tables near train stations.

Covered markets are cleaner and less slippery than street markets. There are two kinds: privately run and publicly funded.

The Hong Kong Housing Authority lets out stalls to individual stall operators through open tender for a fixed period of three years and manages the markets. In June 2017, there were 22 markets, six of which were single-operators[5]. These private markets are located in shopping

---

[5] https://www.legco.gov.hk/research-publications/
     english/1617in14-single-operator-markets-under-the-hong-
     kong-housing-authority-20170601-e.pdf

malls of public housing estates. They are air-conditioned which is ideal in sweaty hot days. They look more like supermarkets in the way the goods are displayed and stalls organised. They are very clean and the floor is dry. They offer 1-hour free parking to their customers who spend a certain minimum amount at their mall and use their car park facilities, e.g.: in Tai Po (Kwong Fuk, Tai Yuen) or Kwun Tong (Kai Tin) or Tuen Mun (Yau Oi), etc. Rents have kept increasing especially after the refurbishing of the venues. People complain that they do not want expensive vegetables coming from Europe and have to travel further from their home to buy cheaper foodstuffs. Fast-food restaurants are located nearby the market area.

The government-funded markets are run under the Food and Environmental Hygiene Department (FEHD). It operates about 80 wet markets in municipal buildings. Close to 30 are on Hong Kong and the outlying islands, 20 on the Kowloon peninsula and 30 in the New Territories. FEHD is planning to renovate public markets and set up cooling devices in one quarter of them that still do not have it. Stalls that used to operate in street markets before 2000 (and were close to the new covered markets) have since then moved into these municipal buildings. The floor is still slippery and you have to be careful particularly in the fish and meat sections. Signs at the entrance of indoor markets, showing a person slipping and falling, warn market-goers of the wet floor. Free wireless internet access service is available in the whole building, like in many government-run facilities.

Cooked-food centres are housed in the same municipal complexes where indoor markets are and provide affordable and fast-food eateries or cha-chaan-tengs. You can buy live fish and other seafood at the market and bring them to these restaurants and they will cook them for you.

Vegetable stalls

When I arrived in Hong Kong in 1986, I was at a loss. I arrived at the end of June when it was the season of gourds. There were many types of "gwa[1]", such as the winter melon, bitter melon, chayote, angled luffa, bottle gourd, fuzzy or hairy melon, yellow cucumber (also called old cucumber), that I had never seen nor tasted before.

Cucumbers were bigger than the French ones and had a smoother skin. The winter melon was quite large and slices were cut upon request. The gourd was supposed to be rich in vitamins and good in summer to cool down the body temperature. Winter melon soup is a classic among locals. However, it needs a lot of flavoured ingredients, such as ginger, dried Chinese mushrooms, dried shrimps and Chinese ham, to enhance its bland taste.

Some green beans were fat and others were so long that they looked like shoestrings. The eggplants were thinner and more elongated than the French ones. Chinese spinach and amaranth were sold with their stalks and hairy roots. The whole plant was tender enough to be cooked in whole,

Piles of green leafy vegetables were stacked high. I did not know most of them,

Now I get it!

baak⁶-choi³

choi³-sum¹

gaai³-laan⁴ ⁽²⁾

but quickly I learnt to recognise the three main ones: bok choy, Chinese flowering cabbage, and Chinese kale.

but local people did not eat it raw. In France, spinach leaves were larger and thicker and the thick leaf stems were discarded and not sold. Carrots were huge and looked like fodder beets and sold without foliage. You could find smaller carrots coming from abroad at the supermarket, but they were still big compared to the European ones.

Piles of green leafy vegetables were stacked high. I did not know most of them, but quickly I learnt to recognise the three main ones: bok choy, Chinese flowering cabbage and Chinese kale. The latter two looked a bit similar at first, but were easy to distinguish once I knew that the first one had yellow flowers and the second white flowers. Bok choy, which was available all year round, looked like the mini version of Swiss chards that my mum used to cook. She either stir-fried the stems or baked the leaves and stalks previously mixed into a béchamel sauce and topped with grated cheese. She also made omelette with the thick green leaves.

Later I could recognise other greens such as: A-choy, watercress, morning glory, amaranth, spinach, pea shoots, Shanghai white cabbage, Ceylon spinach that is colloquially called slippery vegetables, and also garland chrysanthemum, a slightly bitter plant that is good in hotpot. I also discovered the yellow Chinese chives. At first, I had never paid particular attention to the long and flat plant. This veggie is grown in the dark, just like endives and white asparagus, hence its pale colour, and is often added in fillings for rolls and dumplings or served chopped with noodles and stir-fry dishes.

Beetroots were sold raw with the tops unlike in France where vendors pre-cooked the red roots to save customer's time. French cooks just had to peel and slice them to make colourful salads with, for example, hard-boiled eggs and potatoes served with mustard dressing. In Hong Kong, locals did not use them to make salads but soups with both the root and the leaves, without forgetting the meat to add flavour, like in most Chinese soups.

You could find pre-peeled green turnips, carrots and chestnuts, albeit at a slightly higher price. In France, I had never seen carrots that were peeled off – certainly because they would dry out and darken rapidly due to their small size. Only squash is sold with the skin peeled because peeling it even with a very sharp knife is difficult and challenging.

At the end of 1980s, the selection of vegetables at supermarkets was quite small, except in areas with many expatriates. At that time, I lived in Chi Fu Fa Yuen in Pokfulam where the choices were limited to potato, carrot, head cabbage and the tasteless iceberg lettuce. I also recall buying red cabbage and raw alfalfa sprouts. To my surprise, I discovered that alfalfa was quite simply another name for lucerne, the very same nutritious hay which my parents used to grow in our garden for our rabbits! Today each time I see the frail weed-like plant, I also recall the sandwich eatery in Prince's Building in Central where I first ate them. Therefore, it was more than necessary to buy at the market where I could find more choices and fresher goods.

In France, since the early 1990s, oriental vegetables such as bok choy and amaranth can be found at supermarkets specialised in imported fresh goods and groceries. Ten years ago, my friend and her husband who are market producers in France, started growing bok choy and Napa cabbage for sale. French people are very fond of them and they continue to grow the two veggies. They also tried to grow soybeans, but had to give up as it was too difficult to take care of. French people cook them in the same way as bulgur wheat and make tabbouleh salad with the grains.

Today some vegetable stalls in Hong Kong, not only in Central or Eastern districts but also in the New Territories, sell Western vegetables such as endives, artichokes and fennel, albeit at a much higher price than in France. I am not in favour of buying them as I am trying to buy local produce as much as possible. When everybody is talking of greenhouse gases and the effect on our planet, importing vegetables from miles away seems a bit ridiculous. Of course, it is easy for me to say so as I can always travel and taste these delicious veggies when I go to France to visit my relatives.

Meat stalls

Back in 1986, most supermarkets did not sell meat except for those in areas like Stanley or Repulse Bay where more foreigners lived. You had to buy meat at market butchers. There are many differences in the way that meat was sold at markets in Hong Kong and France, the most evident being the way in which meat is presented.

At that time in France, meat stalls operated from mobile shop vans although the regulation was not as stringent as it is today. Today all fresh meat, cold cooked meat and offal must be preserved at 4°C maximum to avoid spoilage. Meat is displayed in window cases per food safety and hygiene standards. Butchers stand behind the window display and customers on the pavement facing them.

It was rather intimidating to see meat stalls in Hong Kong, which were reminiscent of some of the 16th century oil paintings from Peter Aertsen or Annibale Caracci depicting butcher's shops. Chunks of meat hung on metal bars, next to tongues sticking out that looked as if they were making faces at me. On the side pillar hung pale rose air bags (stomachs and lungs) and knuckles with hair. In France, trotters were always cleaned with hair burnt off and certainly would not be displayed at the front of the shop! Even low-priced cuts would be displayed in an attractive way in individual trays, just like the expensive cuts.

In Hong Kong pig's heads, snouts, cheeks, ears and kidneys were set flat on side tables right on the wooden counter. For me, it was not the view of those stalls that was frightening me but rather the unpleasant smell when passing in front, especially in summer time.

Butchers chopped meat on wooden counters that had protruding cutting boards showing deep marks of knife engraved. Red lampshades were diffusing a warm and reddish hallow to make the meat look fresher.

Hong Kong butchers stood both inside and / or outside their stall, in front or behind the table counter, to serve their clients. They did not bother about the presentation and kept a bucket full of unwanted parts, either at the foot of the table counter or on the table in full view of the clients. What I considered an eyesore was very practical for the butchers. Indeed, it was handy to put bloody bones, fat and guts into the container. Waste drips sometimes dropped on to the ground and as a result, the floor was slippery and a strong smell spread all around the facility.

I had sold tripe at markets in Paris' 13th and 20th arrondissement and the view of raw meat and offal did not trouble me at all, but some scenes in Hong Kong seemed surreal. In Hong Kong, there is no dress code. I recall seeing bare-chested butchers and a few even with a cigarette butt resting on their ears! Ooh la la! These scenes would not have been possible in France. But surprisingly there were no flies! In France, butchers have to wear professional outfits: aprons, trousers, jackets and shoes. You can also see butchers wearing knit gloves, the type used by labourers. You must think I am kidding you, but just look around in summer days at the Mongkok market on Canton Road! Some scenes can put you off!

I was also amazed when I witnessed for the first time a butcher cutting a pig carcass on the pavement in front of his stall and trimming fat with his sharp meat cleaver. Today you can still see the same scene even at indoor markets. Butchers carry on with their task without being distracted and are the least bothered by busy passers-by. They do not even seem to care when I take photographs.

One day I even saw a pig head overpassing me in Nelson Street market in Mongkok. What a shock! Another time I saw a young man jumping out of a refrigerated van with a pig carcass slung on his bare back and walking amid the crowd on the pavement to make his delivery to the butchers' on the other side of the street. Locals are used to this practice and do not seem to care at all. At other places which are less crowded like Tai Po, you can see pig carcasses being delivered on trolleys. I could not imagine this happening in France with all our stringent hygiene regulations.

Chunks of meat hung on metal bars, next to tongues sticking out that looked as if they were making faces at me.

Bare-chested butchers are common in Hong Kong, but no way in France.

A butcher cutting a pig carcass.

Pig carcasses being delivered on trolleys.

Today many people are put off by meat stalls in Hong Kong and I know that many of them never buy meat there because they are not sure if it is sanitary enough. The no-frills stalls at the indoor markets are unattractive with their walls clad in toilet-style white tiling and the array of hooks, buckets, plastic bags, fans and red lampshades are equally not appealing. It is also disconcerting that the slabs of red meat all seem similar and do not bear names. However, I always buy meat at wet markets and I have never been sick by the sights, but I can understand if some people cannot stand the view of fresh meat, they are reluctant to get close to butchers'. However, I still follow my mother-in-law's advice and rinse meat and blanch it before cooking it. The primary reason behind the custom is to remove the excess fat, but it also means to remove the impurities. This is a good practice given that the meat is not chilled and is hung in open air. Another local practice is to rinse pork meat before mincing it.

Talking about hygiene and health, Hong Kong encountered a few food scares during the past 30 plus years, for instance pork coming from Mainland China being contaminated (some was said to glow in the dark), swine flu pandemics and repeated bird flu occurrences. Similarly in Europe, eating beef, pork and poultry has not been without worry after the outburst of mad cow disease, swine and bird flu.

Poultry

The poultry section at Hong Kong indoor markets is located far away from other goods. Its isolation is not meant to save us from the chicken's distinctive odour, but it is a soft reminder of the danger that they may cause. In fact, near the entrance there is a poster warning us of the danger of bird flu. This psychological barrier tells me to avoid this area and for that reason, I seldom go there. Since the first human outbreak in 1997, stringent hygiene measures have been put in place to prevent another reoccurrence. Recurring bird flu cases have occurred in the past years and there have been a few bans on the sale of live poultry from the mainland to prevent the import of bird flu virus. A government's proposal for a central slaughterhouse has never been accepted as the Chinese like to eat freshly slaughtered chickens, believing that frozen chickens will lose their original flavour.

Tai Po Hui market has a stall selling two species, the silky or black-boned chicken and Kamei chicken (since 2003) with no added hormones which are bred in Hong Kong. The cockerel is proudly called grand master of the house.

At all stalls, whether in Hong Kong or in France, we can buy whole, half chicken or just parts such as breasts, thighs, legs, etc.

In Hong Kong, you can either wait for sellers to pluck and clean the bird or come back half an hour later to collect it. Chickens are plucked in a washing machine drum look-alike. You can also buy giblets: livers, hearts, gizzards, cockscombs, testicles and claws as well as duck tongues. The Chinese believe that rooster testicles, that go by the culinary name of "chicken-seeds" or "chicken's offspring", will enhance male prowess and they are one of the food items on the menu at hotpot restaurants. In France, "white kidneys", as they are elegantly called, are sold parboiled unless they are pre-ordered. The French like them with a béchamel served in pastry cases called vol-au-vent. Some add cockscombs (which need to be ordered) to combine smooth and gelatinous textures to the creamy sauce. French people stir-fry livers, hearts and gizzards and serve them hot on top of a green salad. In Lyon, we also make a kind of soufflé with chicken liver. However, we don't eat "phoenix claws", the culinary and elegant name of chicken feet! Neither the duck tongue, which Hong Kong people consider a delicacy.

Checking if hens have already laid eggs.

Plucking chicken in France.

Chicken feet are disliked by most foreigners, but I like their texture which is similar to the small cockscombs that I loved when I was small. At that time, my parents found it strange that my favourite parts of the chicken were the neck, brain and crown. Little did I know at that time that I would love the claws that are served at dim sum restaurants. Talking about the chicken brain, my siblings and I used to take turns to eat the tiny-sized brain, and we would keep track of whose turn it was.

I remember when chickens were sold in wooden cages at the street markets on Wanchai Road and its vicinity. I can still visualise the vendors tucking the hens through their arms (the hen facing backward) and their clients, usually elderly women, blowing the rear of the birds. Were they doing a physical examination? Did they want to see the hen's rumps? I know people who are fond of this part. Only later did I know that they were merely checking if the hole of the hens was small or large, the air lifting the feathers and showing their private parts. If the vent was small, it meant that the hen had not laid eggs before and thus it was a young hen and its meat would be tenderer. Recently, a chicken seller in Mongkok told me that if her clients wanted to see by themselves whether the chicken was young or old, she would show them the vent. While explaining this to me, she demonstrated it!

In France, in the 1970s, farmers used to suffocate pigeons discreetly behind their back and chickens were sold live or already slaughtered and plucked if pre-ordered. Today you can't find live poultry anymore at the market.

Strangely you will not find any eggs in the poultry section of Hong Kong markets. In France, chicken farmers sell chicken and quail eggs as well. They sell chicken, ducks and guinea fowls. Most of them sell plucked and cleaned birds in whole or in part. They also sell thick duck breast fillets from force-fed ducks. Force-fed ducks and geese can be ordered. They also sell duck and goose liver to make foie gras and terrine, as well as young goat meat in spring and rabbits.

Talking about rabbits, my parents raised rabbits in their backyard for their meat. Some of my readers might find us French very cruel. Although people usually associate rabbits with carrots, we did not feed them with the orange vegetables but with lucerne that my parents grew specifically for them as well as oats or bran mixed with boiled old potatoes. Whenever we had leftover bread that was too stale to make French toast, we would feed it to them. You should hear them making crunchy noise when gnawing on the hard bread! We kept one female and one male rabbit in separate hutches, but about twice a year we put them together and about twice a year, the female rabbit had a litter of about 8 to 10 kittens, and 6 months later they would be big enough and ready to be sautéed in mustard sauce, a classic recipe, or braised in white wine. I also recall that I helped my mum making rabbit and pork meat terrine. It is quite peculiar that Cantonese people do not eat rabbits as Chinese people would eat almost everything which has four legs, as the saying goes.

Apart from rabbits, my parents also raised backyard hens; though occasionally we bought live poultry: spring chickens and ducks during the year, and either a goose or a turkey at Christmas. My father went to one of the neighbouring farms to get the slaughtered poultry and my mum did the plucking and gutting. I did not mind helping her, but my sister and brother did not like taking part in these activities. I recall once when the farmer had no time to kill the hens that my mum had ordered and my dad brought them back still alive. The delicate task fell on him who had a bit of experience with our home-grown hens. I know he hated doing it. I did not watch the gory scene, but helped submerge the birds in boiling water before pulling their feathers manually. What a chore!

I recall my mum sometimes pan-fried poultry's blood in a saucepan where she had previously fried chopped parsley and onion as per her mother's recipe. The bird was bled dry and its blood was cooked immediately before it had time to coagulate. Blood curds at Hong Kong markets are often made with chicken's or duck's blood. French farmers used to give you the blood of the freshly slaughtered chicken with a bit of vinegar in it to prevent it from clotting. People used to stew the cockerel together with red wine. Similarly, rabbit's blood as well as the liver were also added to make rabbit stew with red wine.

Fishmongers'

The sight of a fish shop is discomforting for some people. Some of my fellow countrymen living in Hong Kong admit that they do not eat seafood at home because they do not know how to cook it. I concede that the gory sight of grass carps being prominently displayed with their hearts still beating slowly and heads moving, fish being gutted and frogs being butchered right in front of you, or rows of cut fish heads with their vitreous eyes looking up could unsettle more than one person. Mud carp or dace (a long grey fish) covered with blood is a common sight at Hong Kong markets. Mounds of minced meat covered with plastic sheet to make the famous fish balls that Hongkongers love can be spotted at many fish stalls. These are definitely not scenes for the fainthearted. My son is one of them. Like many young people, he much prefers supermarkets for their cleanliness. Although his grandma brought him to the market after school to buy pomfret, the seawater fish that he liked so much, his childhood experience did not make him immune to the smelly and unpleasant sights.

Fishmongers'

Hong Kong fish stalls are full of strange things such as live frogs piled up in cages, sea tortoises and soft shell turtles kept in fishing nets! There are fresh abalones from Australia, South Africa and China that I have never had before, their lips still moving and trying to climb over the edge of their basin. French call them "sea truffles" due to their high price and make terrine with them, which they call "Abalone rillettes". Oh, what about those huge geoducks or elephant trunk clams! I love raw oysters, but to my regret locally grown oysters are not meant to be eaten raw; they are sold in batches, pre-shucked and ready to be braised, fried or barbecued. Today you can also find larger fat milky oysters from the USA, also pre-shucked and sold in plastic jars.

Another difference from the French fishmongers is that you can buy live fish and shellfish still wriggling as the Chinese like fresh and moving food. Many species of groupers, some with bright-coloured spotted scales, are kept live in water tanks or styrofoam boxes filled with oxygenated water, waiting for their turn to be fished out and taken away by a client. Each time the fishmonger catches a live fish, the ensuing struggle results in water splashing both the floor and passers-by.

In France, all seafood is immediately stored in flaked ice, as soon as feasible. There are no live shrimps at markets and the crustaceans have a nice orange-pinkish colour because they are cooked right after being caught. In Hong Kong, prawns and shrimps are kept live in water. As the day progresses and their vitality declines, they are moved from their water bucket to metal dishes or spread on the plastic film over a bed of ice. The difference in prices reflects the physical state of the animals and molluscs – the alert ones, those struggling for life and, usually at the end of the day, the motionless.

The first fish name I learnt in Cantonese was grouper, a quite expensive fish that I chose from a fish tank at a seafood restaurant in Lau Fau Shan. However, I did not cook it but the restaurant did. Even today I like to go to the Tai Po Hui market where I can buy a nice live fish and then bring it to one of the restaurants in the cooked-food centre above the market. It is so convenient. I think Cantonese-style steamed fish sprinkled with hot oil, soya sauce and spring onion preserves best the freshness and natural taste of fish. If the fish is big, we will ask for "1 fish – 2 dishes", fillets are stir-fried and the bony parts are either braised with ginger and scallions or steamed.

I had never bought fish myself before coming to Hong Kong. My parents lived far away from the sea and I only had fish once a week, usually on Fridays according to religious tradition. My mum was not familiar with fish and the strong smell in the kitchen deterred her from cooking fish more often. Furthermore, fish was in general more expensive than meat. She used to buy fillets and either blanched them or baked them, served with melted butter and lemon juice topped with chopped parsley. She also bought frozen breaded fish, one of the favourite kid's foods. Occasionally she made squids a la Provençal (stewed with bell peppers and tomatoes) or mussels in white wine.

I could only distinguish shellfish like squids, shrimps, clams and crabs. I could cook squids and clams but not crabs. I do not find eating the famous hairy crabs funny. It gives me lots of troubles for a poor reward. Had I lived close to the seaside in France, I might have been able to recognise more seafood. There were quantities of red, silver and yellow fishes sold in batches on metal plates. Some stalls were specialised in small fish and others in live fish. Furthermore, I did not know how a cod or hake, species commonly found in France, looked like because I had only seen them filleted.

How to choose fish? Of course I could use my common sense and look at the colour of the scales, check if the fish had vibrant colours and clear glossy eyes, but what if I was to be swindled? I felt lost and helpless, even more than at the vegetable stalls or the butchers'. I could not ask where the fish came from. Was it from the sea or river? Was it farm-bred or fished in sea or river? The price would evidently be much affected by these factors. But how could I ask these questions when I could not speak Cantonese?

I was afraid the fish seller would give me a fishy (pun!) fish! The French remove any muddy taste by keeping the fish in salted water for several hours; the Italians do the same and add wine vinegar as this is cheap in their country. I also heard that some people put white vinegar in the fish mouth. The Chinese stir-fry fish with ginger to remove the fishy taste. And what if the fish had too many bones? I did not dare buying fish for many years, which I regret.

Hong Kong fishmongers wear long polyurethane apron and plastic boots due to the wet environment as seafood is kept in water as long as possible, whereas in France market operators work in a dry environment and do not need waterproof protection. French fishmongers sell from mobile market vans and fish, crustacean and mollusc must be stored on flaked ice between 0°C and 2°C. Fish is wrapped in butcher paper and you cannot see any blood. Sometimes sellers like to recover ice with aluminium foil, but in Hong Kong they use a plastic film.

Typical Chinese stalls

Besides fresh or "wet" food, most of the Hong Kong markets have stalls dedicated to South-East Asian foodstuffs as there is a large community of people coming from Thailand, the Philippines and Indonesia. You can also find cut flowers and ornamental fish as well as clothes and goods in the market's "dry" area.

Here are the stalls that do not exist in France.

Tofu stalls

Stalls that sell soybean and gluten products were the most interesting for me. All the goods were new to me. I had never come across the fawn colour rounded-corner cubes (deep-fried bean curd) piled up in wire mesh baskets, nor the white bean curd steaming hot, nor the pale yellow dried bean curd sheets and ribbons. My closest encounter with tofu products had been in Paris' Chinatown where I discovered the white blocks in a bucket full of water and mistook it as cheese in its early making stage and just removed from the strainers. Nor had I ever seen the light beige sausages that are not made with meat but soya beans. They do not taste at all like chicken, but nonetheless are called vegetarian chicken. These are delicious as a cold starter, sliced with cucumber and a garlic soya sauce, or in stir-fries mixed with mushrooms and vegetables.

Neither had I ever heard of gluten as a food before coming to Hong Kong. Nor had I ever seen those brown balls made with wheat gluten that look like huge silkworm cocoons. Gluten foodstuffs are mock meat for vegetarians!

Tofu sellers sometimes sell mushrooms and vegetables. I had tried before straw mushrooms, the Chinese traditional fungus, in canned food, bought from the grocery store in the Chinatown of Paris and am happy to find that fresh ones are much tastier.

Some soybean sellers also sell other weird foodstuffs like salted jellyfish (those transparent yellowish bands), fresh kelp (these dark green ribbons), fish balls and fish cakes.

You can also find different types of pickled greens at their stalls as well as blanched octopus, pig's skin, pork intestine and beef tripe stored in basins of water. The latter four items are much appreciated by locals in hotpot. I was surprised to find pig's blood curds at this stall; as I mentioned before, this food was not sold by pork butchers. Actually the blood might not be from pig but duck or chicken. The jelly and wobbly red-brownish cubes are stored in basins of water and usually served in congee.

Tofu stall

Grocery

Grocers sell dried nuts and grains, Chinese sausages, condiments and preserved food. Dried goods are either sold by weight, or pre-packed for sale to save both clients' and shopkeepers' time. Home-made sauces are stored in 100g-plastic bags, tied with a rubber band and hung on wire racks. They are of the same or even higher quality as pre-packaged branded ones. This is where I buy preserved red bean curd, the reddish creamy curd with a sweet and strong alcohol taste, for making braised pig's trotters with peanuts, and the preserved white bean curd, the cubes that taste like blue cheese, as well as many other items: fermented bean paste, pickled mustard tuber, dried octopus and preserved gizzards for soups, etc.

Some grocers also sell tea leaves and strange-looking things like those dried slugs (sea cucumbers), yellowish and hard pockets (fish swim bladders), or long brownish worms (cordyceps).

You can also find pre-packed dried ingredients which are very handy; you just need to add meat or fish and sometimes vegetables to make soups. Soups are very important for Cantonese people and some require long hours of simmering which, in addition to their nutritional and medicinal values, make them a symbol of love. Grown-ups like to go back to their parents' home to drink soups, as much as their parents like them to come back home to drink soups. Soups in summer are good to keep the body hydrated and some ingredients are said to be able to cool down the body heat. I recall the first Chinese soup I had in Hong Kong in the summer of 1985. At that time, I found it very strange to drink the dark broth and merely touched at the ingredients. Soups in France are not as highly valued as in Hong Kong. My friend who has a farm close to Vienne tried to sell homemade potages with fresh produce, but stopped as there were not enough people interested in buying soups. On the other hand, her homemade jams and fresh fruit juices sell like hot cakes. French like to spread jam on their toast at breakfast but don't have time to make it and homemade jams always taste better than commercial ones.

French markets don't have such type of groceries. Some markets have stalls dedicated to selling spices, or coffee (beans or ground), wine, fresh pasta and potato gnocchi. Handmade pasta is common in the south and south-east of France where the cuisine has a major Italian influence.

Grocery stall

Egg stalls

In Hong Kong, eggs are found both at grocers and specialised stalls. I like to see the way in which the fragile goods are displayed – in large round wicker trays lined with a piece of plastic cloth on a sawdust bed or piled up on a carton in a pyramid shape. Some stalls sell them in cellophane bags of 2, 5, 6, or 7 pieces each, depending on their size. Pungent century eggs (those covered with wood chips and mud) and salted duck eggs (covered with charcoal powder) are wrapped in newspapers.

I recall the first time I saw, in 1986, a lady examining eggs under a light bulb. I wondered what she was doing and learnt later that she was simply checking that there was no embryo inside. Today it is less common to see customers checking if eggs are fresh, but there are always spotlights above the eggs for those who wish to do so. At that time Hong Kong supermarkets sold imported eggs packed in cardboard cartons as well as local eggs. There was also a light bulb and customers used to put the selected eggs in a small plastic bowl and have them wrapped in newspapers at the cashier.

(What was she doing?)
Checking that there was
no embryo inside the egg.

In France, chicken and quail eggs are sold by cheese sellers, chicken farmers and specialised stalls. Farmers humorously call the eggs produced by chickens that have the freedom to run outdoor "happy hen's eggs".

The French do not eat duck eggs and I had never seen in France preserved duck eggs, nor salted duck egg-yolks (those orange balls you can see wrapped in cellophane bags), nor century eggs as in Hong Kong. Chicken eggs are sold by the dozen or half a dozen and displayed on 36-piece egg trays stacked on top of each other. Customers in France bring their own sturdy box to house their six eggs safely, thus avoiding making an omelette on their way back home. I remember when I was small, my mum would bring a blue plastic suitcase-like box to the market. We seldom bought eggs as we had about half a dozen laying hens in an enclosure on my paternal grandma's property about 50 metres away from our house. But at times when our hens did not produce enough eggs, my mum would buy some at the market, especially around the holidays when we received family members and she wanted to make desserts.

During our school holidays, we took turns to go to the chicken coop to feed our chickens with leftovers from our meals and peelings. Very often we also had to complement their feeding with wheat. We also had two dwarf chickens: one hen and one cockerel, a gift from one of my dad's friends. I recall that the cockerel, despite his small size and being the only male in the flock, liked to fight and was quite aggressive and ruled the roost in the coop. The small hen laid lots of tiny delicious eggs, but she was very smart and would try to hide them. She used to sneak out through the wooden gate sticks and hide in the bushes to lay her eggs. We had difficulty in finding her hiding place and if we did not find her nest soon enough, then the eggs would have been wasted. Once during a winter, we found her sitting on her eggs in a shrub. It was snowing and she barely had any protection from the cold wind.

"Happy hen's eggs" – a humorous name for the eggs produced by chickens that have the freedom to run outdoors.

When I was small, my mum would bring a blue plastic box to the market.

About five years ago, after the trend of rooftop vegetable gardens, the "chicken it's cool" ("poule" or hen in French rhymes with cool) campaign helped the rise of non-professional chicken keepers. City councils in France encouraged their citizens to raise backyard chickens in urban areas for the sake of reducing waste. Hens were not expensive and did not require lots of space. Furthermore, not only people could have fresh eggs while reducing food waste, the need of chemicals to treat plants in the vicinity also decreased as chicken ate parasite insects.

Our aggressive dwarf cock ruled the roost in the coop.

hack Sir.

Kack-kaack-kaaack!

Frozen and marinated meat, and fish balls

When temperature drops below 15°C, which is very cold by Hong Kong standard, locals like to make hotpot and you can see queues in front of stalls specialised in fresh noodles, dumplings, chilled and frozen food. Frozen food stalls offer packs of meat already sliced which are very convenient for hotpot. Hotpot is a very convivial dish requiring a minimum of preparation which allows chefs to enjoy food with their guests as each person cooks his / her own food in a soup stock around the dining table. Chinese hotpot is not as rich as the French type of hotpots such as Bourguignonne fondue and Savoyard fondue, the former consisting of deep-frying meat in oil and the latter dipping bread in melted cheese.

Frozen food stalls also sell unpacked marinated meat, beef and fish balls. Hong Kong-style barbecue is one of the favourite activities that people do during the cooler months and in autumn. People buy pre-marinated meat to grill outdoors with friends and relatives.

Marinated meat, beef and fish balls are stored in open freezers. Customers help themselves by seizing the goods with metal tongs and putting them in a plastic bucket pre-wrapped with a plastic bag. The cashier simply turns the bag over, locking the food inside and then closes it. This method allows the bucket to remain clean and ready to be reused immediately. This shows the efficiency of Hong Kong shops.

I am always surprised to see people carrying frozen food in ordinary plastic bag. I hardly see any isothermal bags here.

French markets do not have frozen food stalls at markets.

Medicinal herbs

In Hong Kong, not only the elderlies but also the youths believe in the properties of herbal teas and soups. Vendors take advantage of that belief and will always tell you that such and such produce will benefit you or will do miracle to your skin (i.e. will make you pretty). Those are the magic words for a good sale!

According to Traditional Chinese Medicine, your body condition determines the type of food that you should take and each season has an influence on your body. The notion of "being on fire" or "taking cold" is a concept that all Chinese people are aware of and most believe in. Certain types of food are said to nourish your liver, others your kidneys, while others are better for your spleen. The French don't have this notion, but our grandmothers and some mothers, like mine, believe in the virtue of medicinal herbs and plants such as chamomile, mint and thyme, to name a few.

At some markets like in Mongkok or Tai Po, you can find herbalists selling aloe vera, fresh Chinese olives, banana flowers, weird brown sticks and other plants. Once I bought fresh myrobalans or Indian gooseberries and the herbalist told me that it was good to cure throat inflammation and clear heat. As per his instructions, I made a tea with the bead-like fruit but could not drink the beverage because it was extremely sour. I also tried to pickle Chinese olives as I was told that they could soothe sore throat. The result was disappointing and I much preferred salted tangerines.

Part 4

Differences between French and Hong Kong open markets

Meat

In Hong Kong, beef and pork meat are sold at different stalls; pork butchers just sell pork meat and beef butcher just beef meat, and you can't find terrines or blanched tripe at their stalls. But in France, it is quite common for butchers to sell both meats at the same booth. Furthermore, most French butchers not only sell raw meat but also cooked and cured meat such as terrines, rillettes (meat slowly cooked in fat) and sausages (some filled with offal) as well as marinated skewers and pre-cooked dishes. Some of them also sell poultry and rabbits.

Hong Kong butchers learn from their parents and it is usually a family business, whereas in France butchers shall attend a vocational course and must be professionally qualified to run a shop. France is known for some of the best beef butchers in the world. However, despite not having any formal accreditations, Hong Kong butchers know their trade and are competent. They can give you advice on how to cook and the quantity that you will need for a party of 10, and will even trim off extra bit of fat, slice meat or burn the excess hair off knuckles with a blow torch for the customers. However, they will not go into details as they don't talk much and have to hurry to serve the next client. Nor will they tie a roast. Once I forgot to ask my butcher to debone the pork cheeks and I quickly regretted it. With my blunt knife, I found it not easy at all to debone the abalone meat, which is how Cantonese people called the flesh of the shellfish. I like to cook the cheeks with carrots in red wine.

In Hong Kong, beef butchers sell yellow cattle meat coming from Mainland China. It has a darker colour and tastes stronger than the two main French breeds – Charolaise (white spotless) and Limousine (bright brown). This is one of the reasons why some people prefer to buy meat at supermarkets where they can find imported beef from Australia, Canada or Brazil.

In France, butchers selling beef also sell veal and lamb, and you can find veal roast, veal knuckle, veal blanquette (a cut good for stewing), calf liver, calf brain, calf testicle (elegantly called white kidneys), etc. Calf brain used to be considered a delicacy and was appreciated by Lyon's wealthiest people. Pan-fried calf brain is a traditional Lyonnais dish. My mum cooked brain when I was small and told my siblings and me that it was good for our brain development. Chinese people held the same belief as French, i.e. eating a specific organ will do good to the same human organ. It is not yet scientifically proven and I could not care less about this conviction (maybe I should have!). Perhaps it was a way to attract kids to eat the offal, but I was happy to eat the tiny brains without any enticements. I

97

liked the offal's soft texture and its nutty flavour of brown butter. French parents also tell children to eat carrots so they would have pink thighs or become lovely persons. As if kids do care about it! I heard people saying similar types of things in Hong Kong, such as: if you have strained a muscle, you should eat tendons. I recall that my mother-in-law warned me not to have coffee and soya sauce when I was expecting my son for fear that the black liquids would darken my baby's skin. Both beliefs are not yet proven either.

Pork butchers in Hong Kong outnumber beef butchers. Some sell a variety of black pork that is bred locally, and their stalls are easily recognisable with big posters showing the bulky animals and black-hoofed pig trotters and pig heads with black bristles hung on the stall's side pillars.

Ah! Do you know that French people eat horse meat? I have never eaten horse meat in my life. Horse meat is said to have nutritional value, but its consumption is very tiny and highly controversial. Horse meat butchers are rare and not all markets have one.

In France, you can buy goat meat at halal butchers' which one can usually find in areas where there is a large Muslim population, like in Vienne. The Saturday market has a few stalls manned by butchers originally from North Africa and a halal rotisserie as well. In Hong Kong, there are hardly any market stalls that are specialised in selling halal meat.

My friend in France remembers when her father used

to sell live young male goats at the market in the 1970s. Her parents raised dairy goats to make cheese and only kept the female kids. Whoever bought live goats had to know how to cut their throats! Times have changed, but you can still buy spring goat meat at the chicken farmer's stalls.

Similarly, French sheep farmers used to sell live sheep directly to customers, mainly Muslims who like to roast the whole animal to celebrate the end of Ramadan. The poor things were often slaughtered at their home. Today sheep and goats have to be killed at a central slaughterhouse and according to the clients' religious rites.

Opening hours

Hong Kong: outdoor or covered wet markets stalls are open every day from about 7:00 am to 8:00 pm. It reflects the efficiency and dynamism of Hong Kong. Vendors are spending more than 10 hours per day in their stall, and sometimes 7 days a week.

France: outdoor markets are temporary and usually held once a week for half day. Some open for half day, from 7:00 am to 1:00 pm on each day of the week, except Monday. Luxurious types of covered markets – operating more like a shopping centre – are open all day long for up to 6 days a week (Monday closed).

Price tag display

Hong Kong: markets are "wet" and it is no surprise that besides cardboard, styrofoam is the most commonly used material. Fishmongers only use the waterproof signs. Just observe and check the large quantity of tags with colourful marked prices that are stocked at the back of their stalls and some floating on top of water buckets where fish or shellfish are kept live.

France: signs in France are very informative: not only do they tell you the name of the product but also its origin, variety and size. The information is usually written on a cardboard or plastic tag, or even on a chalkboard. Some tags mimic French lined paper that is reminiscent of primary school notebooks. I love the plastic butchers' tags that carry a picture of a cow or pig and rotating numbers.

Who shops at the open market and why?

Hong Kong: customers buy food for necessity and know they can find goods that are cheaper at wet markets than at supermarkets.

I seldom see young kids there and it is mostly an adult place with middle-aged women and men as well as elderlies. Working women in Hong Kong prefer to go to the markets which are operated by private companies. These newly renovated indoor markets have air-conditioning and are cleaner, looking more like supermarkets. Their floor is not "wet" at all. However, food there is often more expensive as rent is higher than other government-run or street markets.

In Hong Kong, the apparent lack of hygiene might be the primary reasons deterring some people from going to the market. Whenever I talk about going to the market, people are surprised as most of them do not go. At first, I thought they were kidding, but it is actually true. Most of them prefer shopping at supermarkets and some do not actually go themselves but send their domestic helpers. It is true that markets close earlier than supermarkets and working people usually wear shoes that are not comfortable to walk with on slippery floors.

Some people whom I know do not buy seafood at wet markets because they cannot stand the sight of live fish struggling and flying from their tank. Another reason why people do not like wet markets is the bad smell, particularly when you walk past the butchers'. It is indeed a strong deterrent!

France: going to the market is a good way to end the week. One can relax, get some fresh air and recharge one's batteries as most markets are held on Saturday mornings. People like to take time to do their shopping at the market and enjoy talking and meeting with their friends there. They like to have a drink at a cafe nearby; sit around tables and put the world to rights. It is more pleasant and less stressful to shop at markets than at supermarkets, except when it rains or the weather is too hot. Market-goers can walk leisurely among the stalls. At Saturday markets, parents bring along their young kids. Goods are not necessarily cheaper but of good quality, and you can find good deals at the greengrocers.

Michelin-starred chefs often visit local markets to get inspiration. For instance, chef Patrick Henriroux of La Pyramide, a local gastronomic restaurant, does his shopping at the Saturday market in Vienne and buys some vegetables and fruits at my friends' stall. The former owner of La Pyramide in Vienne was Ferdinand Point, the renowned chef and father of modern French cuisine.

Displays

Hong Kong: the overall feeling is "piles" and "quantity". Every little space is fully utilised. Both outdoor stalls and indoor shops are packed with personal items such as rice cookers, umbrellas and thermos as vendors spend most of their time there. Some vendors cannot leave their stalls unattended and thus will have their lunch in their booth. Very often when I go to my vegetable seller early in the afternoon, she is eating straight out of her styrofoam box on a low stool behind her stall and I can only see the top of her head behind the heap of Chinese kale. She can only take a short break to fill up her stomach at this hour when the flow of customers has reduced.

In Hong Kong: the overall feeling is "piles" and "quantity". Every little space is fully utilised.

France: presentation is very important; it has to be attractive. Compared to Hong Kong, displays are rather flat and scattered. Garden farmers display their produce on wooden tables and spread them in a way to give more visibility to their goods, thus more chances for passers-by to see them, stop and eventually make a purchase. Some vendors like to have elegant stalls and skirt the trestle tables with a piece of cloth that matches the colour of their canopies. Others who sell dried products like honey and walnuts prefer to garnish their tables with a piece of red and white checked tablecloth (very French!) or a piece of wax cloth which is easier to clean.

In France: the displays are rather flat and scattered.

Stalls

Hong Kong: there are three types of booths: cubicles, small shops and large stores.

- Cubicles – like those in Graham Street: those have been standardised for safety reasons and the metal kiosks are painted in bright green, orange or yellow. Sun umbrellas and tarpaulin are put in between each stall to give protection from the rain, sun, water dripping from air-conditioning units and anything that might fall from above, for example garments hung on window grilles or bamboo poles from the buildings lining the street. Roof extensions stretching on both sides of the booth and from the front of the booth up to the middle of the lane make the small cubicles look much bigger than their actual size and are handy places to hang things up too. The metal shelters form a covered walkway and in summer it feels like a furnace.
- Small shops: they are family-run businesses and often located in run-down buildings. The sellers

stand inside the shop with their vegetables displayed in front of them on makeshift tables set on the pavement. At peak hours, extra sellers are on duty standing on the pavement to speed up the service. One of their distinctive features is the peeling paint on dark and dirty walls brightly lit with white neon lights. The walls are covered with paper notes and handwritten phone numbers, probably those of suppliers'. A metal curtain serving as a door is lowered at the end of the day.

– Large shops: some belong to a chain of greengrocers and they have a few employees. Customers can physically go into the shops. The shops look more like overcrowded stockrooms and have no door nor decoration. Some shops have a fancy setting, such as the one I saw in Wanchai with its walls covered from floor to ceiling with fake vegetation.

France: there are also three types of booths, quite different from those in Hong Kong:

– Trestle tables: the displays of market gardeners are more elaborate than greengrocers'.

– Market vans: their displays are more elaborate and some are quite attractive.

– Shops: indoor market stalls look more like luxurious shops.

Time allocated to market shopping

🇭🇰 Hong Kong: customers don't spend too much time shopping at stalls. They do not like to waste time and don't like to wait for their turn to be served.

🇫🇷 France: French customers do not mind being served at a slower pace and like to talk with vendors, thus you need more time to do your shopping. They like to know where the produce comes from and are curious about the quality of the crop and farming conditions. For example, they like to know when new potatoes will be picked, when the tomatoes will be ripened and when they will be able to buy the first crop of peas.

Market gardeners are proud to share their passion and knowledge on farming with their clients. Each one has his / her personal style and personality, and a certain sense of humour. They don't mind if you ask them questions. Shoppers need to be patient and wait for their turn.

Live animals

Hong Kong: you can find live frogs, seafood and chicken.

France: markets don't sell live animals (goats, lambs, ducks and chickens) anymore. If you see live animals, they are there only on display to attract clients. For example, in Châtillon-sur-Chalaronne (Ain department) a wandering entertainer plays barrel organ with Brahma cocks swaggering next to him. The breed is the largest in the world, weighing up to 5.5 kg and hens up to 4.5 kg.

Delicatessen

🏵 Hong Kong: there are no booths selling ready-made dishes to take away. Chinese style rotisserie shops selling roasted and marinated meat (siu-mei) made from meat or offal (lo-sui) are present at some markets. Street hawkers used to sell curry fish balls and other hot snacks close to market area. Today indoor markets include a cooked-food centre where shoppers can eat on the spot.

🇫🇷 France: there are more and more caterers who cook dishes right in the market to take away. Fishmongers and butchers also sell ready-made dishes. Indoor markets have brasserie-type restaurants.

Food tasting

Hong Kong: there is no food tasting. It is true that there are not many foods that can be eaten straight at the market as they are uncooked. But what about barbecue pork? I would not mind tasting a bit of it! In fact, local people in general know the taste of roasted and marinated meat and the quality is quite standard. There is no need for sellers to attract new clients.

France: you can taste olives, cheese, bread, cakes and other regional specialties. Tasting is a predictable technique to win clients at French markets. Each cheese tastes differently, depending on its age, the season and the way in which it was made. It can happen that cheese in the same batch tastes differently.

Environmental hygiene

Hong Kong: floor is wet and slippery, particularly in the meat and fish areas. Outdoor markets are located in narrow streets between rows of high-rises. Drops of water often fall from the above air-conditioning units hung on the facades of buildings. Indoor markets are cleaner and some are air-conditioned, but the odour of meat and fish is more pungent than at outdoor markets.

Since 2003 (and following SARS epidemic), stall owners at FEHD-run markets must thoroughly clean up their stalls once a month.

France: floor is dry (except when it rains!). Located on the village plaza or in the city centre, indoors or outdoors, people walk leisurely. Markets in small towns and villages are held at the same place once a week, but in large towns smaller markets are held on each day of the week, except Mondays, at different locations.

Scales

Hong Kong: mechanical scales and digital scales are only checked by inspectors when complaints are made. Vendors who are found to use a defective scale face a fine of about HK$1,000. I like the digital hanging scales that some fishmongers and butchers in Hong Kong use today because it removes any fear of being cheated. They are precise and clients can easily look up at the weight and price.

France: most of the mechanical scales have been replaced in mid-1990s by digital ones. All weighing devices are subject to an annual control and a green label is affixed to the scale once they are properly calibrated. Sellers who use faulty scales are subject to a fine of 450 euros or an administrative sanction.

Payment methods

Hong Kong: electronic payment at wet markets has just been introduced. Since October 2017, the 43 stalls at Po Tat market in Kwun Tong are equipped with an online payment provider. Customers can scan the QR code displayed in the stalls to make payment via their mobile phones. Not many people are using it yet and I wonder if market-goers are ready to get eWallet as people who patronise wet markets are not the young and I.T. expert types. Elderlies and housewives might have smartphones, but they still prefer to pay with cash. But anyway I think we will very soon have to start using this payment method.

Many stalls in Hong Kong are refusing to accept small coins (10, 20 and 50 cents). The reason is two-fold: first, it takes too much time to count them and second, some Hong Kong banks are charging around HK$2 to change coins into notes. I think this is ridiculous because all coins made by the Hong Kong Government are legal tender under the Hong Kong law, and it is illegal to refuse legal tenders. But nobody cares enough to point it out.

Stallholders keep coins and bills in plastic buckets hung with a pulley-like system. Cheques have always been a rarity in Hong Kong and I have never paid by cheque at any shops, even less at market stalls.

Only the shops that sell more expensive food, such as frozen meat, have a cash register and will automatically give you a printed receipt. Other stalls do not use a calculator and if you ever need a receipt, just ask the sellers and they will fill in a printed receipt by hand or simply write the total amount paid on a blank paper bearing their company chop.

▌ ▌ France: don't bring large-denomination bills. Small coins as well as personal cheques are accepted for payments over 10 euros, especially if you are a regular customer. Sellers use a money-belt or a cash register to store the cash they receive from customers. They have to be very careful not to lose sight of their cash register, especially when they are packing up unsold goods and folding trestle tables at the end of a busy and tiring morning. Though each transaction is rather small, the accumulated sum might represent quite a substantial amount of cash at the end of the day!

Most stalls give you a receipt.

Prices

Hong Kong: goods at markets are usually cheaper than at supermarkets.

France: goods at markets are not always cheaper than at supermarkets. Local producers are not particularly cheap, but customers know where the products come from and are ready to pay a bit more. Greengrocers offer better prices, but you have to buy in large quantities. You can ask for a smaller quantity, albeit at a slightly higher price per unit.

Rental

🏵 Hong Kong: it is not clear what the exact monthly rental for a stall managed by FEHD is. Booth allocation is made through open auction and rent prices vary a lot. Rental is set below market rate, which is good for consumers as highlighted in the South China Morning Post in September 2018.

🇫🇷 France: getting places at most popular markets in France is difficult and candidates are selected by lucky draw. Vendors subscribe for a fixed place for a period of time. Those who do not have a fixed account can rent a vacant place whenever it becomes available, but at a higher cost given the shorter term of lease. Prices also depend on the spot and city. Like in Hong Kong, a location in the city centre is obviously more expensive than on the outskirt. Indoor market stalls close to the entrance or with high traffic are worth more than a booth which is far away from the main passage and difficult to access. In Paris, the rental price per day for a fixed outdoor place is about 4.05 Euros per metre and in a good location in Vienne 1.5 Euros per metre. Places in Reunion, the French overseas territory, is said to be even more expensive than in mainland France.

Bargaining

Hong Kong: you can try bargaining at Hong Kong markets, but there is no guarantee that it will work! In general, Hong Kong shoppers don't haggle, but they get a few complimentary stems of spring onion each time when they buy greens.

France: people are not used to bargaining. Some vendors do not mind rounding down the price for a few cents, but some have no such practice. Others like to give away free fruit or vegetables when the market is closing, albeit not the best looking ones. Some prefer to add a bit more veggies on top of our bags.

Containers

🏵 Hong Kong: veggies are loaded in styrofoam boxes, wire-mesh circular trays, red sieve bowls, wicker baskets.

🇫🇷 France: dark green or red plastic basins are replacing the old-fashioned white metal basins and the grille-like walls allow air to circulate and water to drain, similar to the wash basins ever-present at Hong Kong markets. The old-fashioned lightweight 4-feet rectangular wooden crate (we both use cageot-masculine and cagette-feminine) that can be stacked up endlessly and allows air to circulate is still in use, but coloured plastic ones are now more noticeable. French greengrocers do not bother much with the presentation and very often their goods are just left in their original packages.

About the vendors

Hong Kong: the name of the stall, usually printed in red characters, suffices as customers know where to find the vendors: they are there every day! Often shops' names have auspicious meaning that is supposed to bring luck and hence flourishing business.

France: French producers put large signs on tarpaulin bearing their stalls' name, address and contact number. Some vendors have slogans printed on the top of their vans or on the tarpaulin at the back of their stalls that rhyme with their company name such as "Chez Pascal on se régale" meaning "At Pascal's we enjoy food."

Light and air-conditioning

Hong Kong: the number of lights, particularly the butchers', can be quite impressive. The red shadows diffused to the heap of goods presented below are meant to highlight their freshness. The meat is no longer reddish brown but pinkish! Today LED PAR lights have almost replaced the traditional incandescent and fluorescent light bulbs and lampshades are not necessarily red.

As Hong Kong summers are humid and very hot, it is much more comfortable to shop at air-conditioned indoor markets. However, about one quarter of the government-run markets are not equipped with air-conditioning as they are in old buildings. Not only in summer but also in winter, keeping low temperature is necessary to ensure good ventilation, prevent spreading of germs and refresh the smelly environment. Both indoor and open-air markets' stallholders use fans to ventilate the hot stuffy air and cool down the temperature.

France: not many public places have air-conditioning, but we do not have the same stuffy atmosphere. The weather is drier and generally more comfortable. Whenever possible, we prefer to open windows. Electric fans are not common either. When winter comes, it can be very cold but in some cities, such as Vienne, electric heaters are strongly prohibited for fear of overloading the circuit and not having enough power supply for the sellers' electronic scales. Portable gas heaters are accepted, but gas cylinders are heavy, costly and need to be handled with care, so sellers limit their usage. Similarly, vendors restrict the use of light as much as possible as they want to avoid any power shortages that could halt the weighing of goods and cause a detriment to their business. In the eyes of sellers, one of the disadvantages of outdoor market stalls is that it is not easy to find suitable places to hang the spotlights other than on the canopy ribs.

Weather

Outdoor stallholders are courageous as they sell in all weathers. They don't like rainy weather as there will be fewer customers.

Hong Kong: it might never be very cold in winter, but in summer hot days last for many months. When there is a typhoon, people don't go outdoors and prices will increase quite substantially as greens have been damaged by heavy rain.

France: Sellers don't like it when temperature drops. Veggies are sensitive to cold temperatures, for instance, potatoes start to freeze at -5°C. During cold spells, prices of greens increase.

Etiquette

Touching the food

For sure, it is easier to buy vegetables and fruit than meat and fish. You can select veggies and put them in a plastic wash basket without any need to talk. In Hong Kong, unlike in France, customers can touch fruit and vegetables before buying and pick the produce they like. French sellers do not like people touching their fruit and vegetables, and it is customary to hear customers asking, "can we touch?" and vendors often replying: "we don't touch!"

In Hong Kong, I have seen people pressing on pork belly slabs with their fingers, checking the freshness of the meat to see whether its texture was moist but not slimy, soft and not tough. I cannot imagine this scene at French markets. I have seen people smelling prepacked meat at supermarkets but never touching fresh meat at the butchers'. At the fish stalls, you sometimes have to pick up your catch yourself and give it to the fishmonger who is standing next to the scale. A towel is hanged on the side pillar for you to wipe your fingers afterwards.

French sellers do not like people touching their fruit.

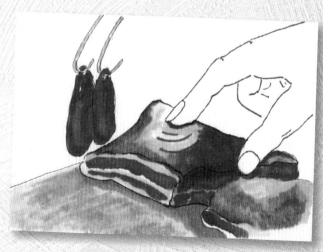

In Hong Kong, people press on pork belly slabs with their fingers to check its freshness.

Courtesy

Hong Kong people are fast and don't talk as much as French do when buying goods at the market. They don't speak a full sentence, but rather state their order in two or three words. French people like using polite forms all the time: "May I have this and that, please?", "Thank you". In Hong Kong, those words are omitted because they are considered to be redundant.

French shoppers always say "hello" before buying, and sellers will ask "will that be all?" before announcing the total amount due in order to make sure that their clients do not want anything else.

Patience

In France, customers need to be patient as vendors like to talk with their clients and take more time to complete an order. You usually make eye contact with sellers so that they know you want to buy. In Hong Kong, people do their shopping in a hurry. At first I patiently waited at the stall, but people arriving after me did not care if there were customers already waiting to be served before them and would just ask the vendor what they wanted or simply handed the veggies that they had selected over to the vendors to weigh.

I recall the first time when I was waiting to be served at the pork butcher's and people did not wait for their turn but overtook me. There were already a few people at the booth when I arrived and I had no idea who had come first. I stood behind what seemed to be a queue and waited for my turn. Suddenly one woman stepped in front of me and asked for a meat cut without the least embarrassment. I immediately asked right after her for HK$10 of lean pork, intending to make my point that it was not her turn. But the butcher did not seem to care and served the woman first. I was furious but did not dare say anything. Then while he was chopping the ribs on the wooden work station with his sharp cleaver, a man arrived, stood next to me and asked something in a loud voice. The butcher handed the meat in a plastic bag to the woman while taking the few coins she was holding out to him, and then turned around and grabbed a slab of meat. I thought he was taking care of my order, but to my surprise I saw him rinsing and mincing meat. This was definitely not my order! This was the second time that someone had overtaken me! How annoying! Finally, my turn came and I hastened to repeat for the third time: "HK$10 of lean pork!!!"

This does not mean that French people never do that – they also do the same – but they will be looked unfavourably on by the people who arrive at the stall before them. The latter will not hesitate to express their dissatisfaction in a polite manner, yet still loud enough so that everyone around can hear the remark and the culprits will feel guilty and hopefully learn their lesson.

Buying meat was quite challenging for me and for many years, I had an apprehensive feeling whenever I went to the butcher's. Not only did I need to make sure to use the right intonation so that I would be properly understood, I also had to act like locals. Over the years I have learnt that in order not to be overtaken by other people, I have to talk loudly when I think it is my turn and above all have to stand close to the counter; otherwise you will never get served.

I stood behind what seemed to be a queue and waited for my turn.

1 catty of pork ribs

Suddenly one woman stepped in front of me and asked for a meat cut without the least embarrassment.

1/2 catty of minced pork

Then a man arrived, stood next to me and asked for something in a loud voice.

$10 of lean pork

After being overpassed twice, I learnt my lesson and hurried to place my order.

Bring your own bag

In France, more and more goods, particularly fruit and vegetables that don't need wrapping are put into the clients' shopping bags at their request. Since January 2017, disposable and biodegradable plastic bags are forbidden in France and stronger bags that are three times costlier (for the vendors) than the thinner ones are provided to clients. Customers are expected to re-use them.

A long time before plastic bags appeared and started to invade our home and planet, customers in France already brought their own shopping bags. My mum recalls using those large black oil-cloth totes similar to the famous Tati striped ones, as well as the string mesh shopping bags that all ladies kept in their handbags in the 1960s and 1970s. The latter were foldable, lightweight and reusable, but they could not carry too many things and small things could pass through the mesh of the nets. I remember when I was small, my mum carried her shopping in a large wicker basket. Everybody had one. Later the rigid type was replaced with a supple version, made with palm leaves and leather handles. We can still see these beautiful handmade pieces, but they are slowly being abandoned for lighter environmental bags and shopping trolleys. The granny's cart has been rejuvenated and younger people are now pushing them. They might be very useful but they are so annoying! Like in Hong Kong, you have to be careful of not letting the wheels of these vehicles step on your toes and hurt you.

I recall when Hong Kong vendors tied up veggies with a type of grass and simply wrapped a pack of bok choy or a piece of meat in newspaper and tie it up with wicker threads. Shall we go back to these days for the sake of environmental protection?

In Hong Kong, meat and seafood are thrown directly into plastic bags, but in France, butchers and fishmongers wrap meat and fish respectively in butcher paper before putting them in a plastic bag.

Part 5

Similarities between French and Hong Kong markets

Tradition

In France, shopping at the market is a tradition. Clients go to the same vendors who have been selling at the same marketplace for three or four generations. Vendors know their clients by their first names. Vendors' kids start to help out at the market stalls on school holidays when they are big enough. French people feel a strong connection with markets, their history, friendliness and good foodstuffs.

In Hong Kong, markets have a long tradition too. However, it seems that they are losing their appeal, as youngsters tend to prefer supermarkets.

Good location & more choices

Markets are conveniently located and you can find fresh products and more choices than at most supermarkets.

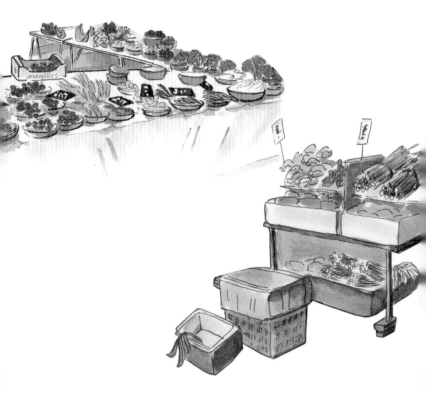

No-fuss places: noise, crowd & flattery

Both in France and Hong Kong, outdoor markets are no-fuss places where people speak loudly and interact. They are lively places full of smiles, friendship and laughter and where people from all walks of life and ethnicity do their shopping.

I had the opportunity to see the market from another perspective when I worked part-time for a tripe seller in Paris. I enjoyed selling and seeing customers coming back each week and chatting with us. I recall my lady boss giving her famous sweetbreads and mushrooms in white cream recipe to her regular clients, and kids being curious or disgusted on seeing calf brains or a beef tongue. I liked the mid-morning break we took in turns when the flow of customers had dwindled and before a new wave of customers came. During that short rest, I would enjoy a hot croissant that my boss bought at the nearby bakery. In the winter, I went to the nearest cafe to get a hot espresso to warm myself up, but could not dawdle and had to come back quickly to take care of the people already waiting patiently for their turn.

French sellers, mainly the greengrocers, like to shout to attract customers and use slogans such as, "Come on, come on, ladies!" "Enjoy the best prices, ladies!" or "See my nice tomatoes!" or "Look at my handsome cauliflowers!" Some like to charm their clients with pleasant remarks and joke around. Others like to shout their best prices at the top of their voice "2 euros each box!" Some customers, particularly men, enjoy sexist comments, such as the ravioli vendors with its catchphrase: "Eat my ravioli and your nights will be crazy!" Ravioli (ravioles) rhymes with crazy (folles). A few sellers like to flatter their clients and call them "little lady" or "young man". You can often hear them asking, "that will do young man?" You can also hear, less often though, old-fashioned sellers calling women "beautiful Germaine." Germaine was a common female name in the 19th century. Another common slogan is "if you find this cheaper elsewhere, I give you a kiss".

In Hong Kong, sellers like to flatter female shoppers and call them "leng^3-nui^2"[6] or pretty girl. Some outdoor stalls are quite noisy and play tapes over and over again to attract customers. It makes you feel like being at a fair where peddlers use microphone and demonstrate how to use new kitchenware and gadgets in front of a large audience. The very loud tape keeps repeating the same

---

[6]   Change of tone from 5 to 2.

slogan: "Gaai¹-fong¹! Gaai¹-fong¹! Today our stall (name of the stall) is doing a promotion! 10 dollars for 4 bundles, 10 dollars for 4 bundles!" Gaai¹-fong¹ is the name given to people living in the same neighbourhood.

Like in France, most sellers like to joke and make fun of people. Here is a funny story that happened to a Hong Kong man who was not a regular market-goer. When walking past a fishmonger, he saw a large fish liver, as big as the plate on which it was displayed, and he wondered how heavy it could be. He had no intention to buy it, but just out of curiosity he stopped and asked the seller. To his surprise, the fishmonger replied, "If I knew the weight, I would not need a scale!" The repartee did not offend the man at all; on the contrary it made him reflect on his silly question. People who want to buy will ask for the price, but not the weight.

French sellers like to shout slogans such as: "if you find this cheaper elsewhere, I give you a kiss".

Holiday

In both France and Hong Kong, stallholders don't take long holidays.

Is there any particular time when Hong Kong stallholders take leave? At first I thought stalls never closed, but yes they did. Wonder how I discovered an unusual phenomenon in a city full of energy that never seems to sleep?

This was at the end of January 1987 and it was going to be my first Chinese New Year in Hong Kong. The day before the first day of this important and long festival, my husband urged me to return home early so that we could go together to the market to buy food before the festival. I arrived home at 4:00 pm, thinking that we would have plenty of time as stalls usually closed at around 7:00 pm. When we arrived at the market, I immediately felt that something was wrong when I saw sellers busy cleaning their stalls. I could not see any vegetables but only empty crates and tables. My husband looked at me and said in a serious voice: "We should have come earlier", meaning that I should have listened to him. I felt bad but it was too late. I had been in Hong Kong for over 6 months and had never seen market stalls close so early before. The city was suddenly so quiet. This was at the end of January and suddenly it was like being in France in August when you wanted to buy bread and could not find any bakery open. In France, most retailers take their annual leave in August. We rushed to the supermarket and had to make do with the remaining bad-looking veggies. Fortunately, we did not have to cook much during the holiday as we were being invited to dine at relatives' place when we paid them the New Year's visit. We ate lots of auspicious dishes such as "braised shiitake mushrooms with lettuce" as the pronunciation of lettuce sounds like "life and money". We were also offered sweets, nuts and various cakes. I tried for the first time the traditional brownish glutinous rice "year cake" and the soft turnip cake with bits of Chinese sausage and dried shrimps in it. Some people are good at making these treats and each year they steam many cakes not only for themselves but also for distribution to friends and relatives before the holiday. No wonder I had seen heaps of white roots at the market the week before! I liked turnip cake immediately, but it was until 20 years later that I learnt how to make it.

This is how I learnt that Chinese New Year was such an important festival that market stalls would close all together for at least 4 or 5 days. Wow! I could not believe that suddenly there would be no place where we could buy fresh food for so many days. Not even the supermarkets were open (at that time). But it made sense to close because business was not going to be good anyway as people could do without shopping for a few days. They had had so much during the celebration and might have leftovers. Nowadays most of the stalls do not stay closed for that long and some will even resume their business as early as on the second day of the Chinese New Year.

We rushed to Pokfulam but villagers were already busy cleaning their stalls.

My husband was not pleased and I felt bad, but it was too late.

We rushed back to Chi Fu Fa Yuen, only to find that the supermarket shelves were almost empty.

In France, the majority of employees enjoy 5 weeks of annual paid leave and August is the favourite holiday month. When everything is closed, why not holidaying as everybody else? Even though market stallholders don't operate each day, they do take some leave and skip a few market days per year, indeed mostly in August because they know their clients will be on holiday too.

Greengrocers can take longer holidays if they wish to, as they only do the selling and don't grow plants themselves. However they do fear that if they take a long absence, customer might go to another vendor for good. As for the market gardeners, their vegetables do not stop growing in August just because most people are on leave. Vegetables need to be harvested and some cannot be stored for a long time, thus producers cannot take extended holidays and can only allow themselves a few days of holiday.

Cheating

Both in Hong Kong and France, most sellers are just a little bit dishonest and will round up the weight to their advantage, but there exists some who are unacceptably deceitful. Obviously the latter are not expecting their customers to come back. Some sellers will press heavily on the scale when you are not looking. In France, you have to be aware of sellers who sell seasonal produce and whom you are unlikely to see again such as those selling wild mushrooms in autumn; they are good at deliberately pressing heavily on the scale to add extra weight.

Some sellers are good at deliberately pressing heavily on the scale to add extra weight.

Rip-off is also common in France with products which are claimed to be locally made but are actually not, especially highly valued local products like olive oil, honey, and homemade cold meats.

Discounted prices at the end of the day

Both in France and Hong Kong, some sellers prepare bunches of goods at the end of the day to get rid of everything left in their stall. You can get better prices, but the veggies will not be the best and the freshest. However, most of the vendors do not like this practice as they fear that their customers might not buy from them again if part of the goods are bad. They prefer to offer smaller quantities at a higher quality.

In Hong Kong, it is also common, especially at the end of the day, to find withered veggies sold at cheaper prices, but clients are aware of it and they don't see this as a big problem.

Overall, shoppers spend less at the market as they are not tempted to buy unnecessary things, as in a supermarket.

Part 6

Advantages of shopping at the open market

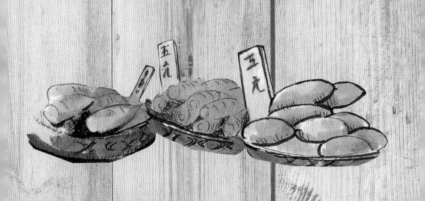

Food quality

Freshness is important. I recall one occasion when I had to throw away most of the content of a pack of lettuce bought at the supermarket because I was not able to see the rotten leaves hidden in the plastic wrapping. In the end I was left with just half of the original quantity and was very unhappy. To whom I could complain?

Market vendors will not sell you bad veggies unless they don't know you and are bad vendors. They are more concerned about the quality and retaining their clients. As everyone knows, "it takes time to build up clientele but does not take long to lose it."

In France, local produce means fresher goods that have been harvested ripe and not been kept in boxes for a long time. In addition, buying from market gardeners in France is better for our health, the community at large and the environment. Most farmers are doing sustainable farming which uses recycling methods and natural energy to better protect our environment.

While only less than 10% of farms produced organic produce in 2016, this number increased by 13.7% within one year, representing 8.3% of the total number of French farms. (Source: Agence Bio).

Moreover, it seems that people who buy at the market are more inclined to cook and will eat healthier. They will not buy ready-made dishes or canned food, and eat out less.

Local and seasonal produce

In France, local farmers sell their vegetables at markets and sometimes at local cooperatives. Vegetables at supermarkets come from large producers, from France or foreign countries and clients don't know how they have been treated. Market-goers like to see and meet the producers behind the products (not only greens but cheese, charcuterie and meat). They like to support farmers who grow their own produce and sell directly to customers as locally grown produce tastes better. France produces more than half of its own need in fruit and vegetables. Some farmers come to the market to sell whatever they have, sometimes it may be only a few crates of salads or apples from their orchards.

At traditional French markets, local farmers outnumber greengrocers. French people tend to dislike the latter because they are importing produce from Morocco, Spain and Central Europe at cheaper prices due to bad economic situation in those countries. Although French people complain about this unfair practice which is detrimental to local farmers, their wallets speak louder than their hearts.

In Hong Kong, local farmers who practise conventional farming sell to wholesalers' associations. Most of the vegetable stalls are run by greengrocers and many produce comes from Mainland China. Only a few of the new generation of market farmers who grow organic produce sell directly to consumers.

At times, you can see elderlies selling food on the pavement near crowded areas like near Tai Po Hui indoor market or train stations in the New Territories. They are happy to sell a few home-grown vegetables, gourds or some medicinal herbs etc. This activity is more like a hobby than a business.

Tofu products, blood curds, sauces and condiments are sometimes locally made, but there is no indication showing what they are. Only pre-packed produce has a label indicating their country of origin.

What is in season? In Hong Kong, it is sometimes quite difficult to say. Take bok choy for instance: it is found all year round as there are different varieties and the leafy vegetable withstands cold and warm temperatures. Furthermore, many veggies are nowadays grown in greenhouses. However, if veggies are grown in Hong Kong, there are two seasons. The cold period, from September to April, is best for Chinese kale, Chinese lettuce, tomato, oriental radish, white turnip and spinach. Gourds, cucumber, eggplants and sweet potato are best during the hot season, from May to August.

In France, we have four seasons. In case you forget, just have a look at the stalls manned by local producers and their products will remind you of Nature's rhythm and will tell you when tomatoes, green peas, new potatoes etc. are in season. You will not find cherries in winter and pumpkin in summer!

More choices

At markets, there is a wider selection for the same kind of food. Another advantage of wet markets in Hong Kong is that you can find vegetables that supermarkets do not sell. For example, I discovered sweet potato leaves, stem lettuce, Chinese box thorn-wolfberry, silver-silk flowering Chinese cabbage and wild rice shoots. I also found at a small stall on Argyle Street in Mongkok a cute-looking gourd called "mouse melon" because its shape and colour look like a small rodent with greyish hair. At the same place I also found pumpkin shoots, Eastern bracken ferns, dragon fruit cereus flowers, purple long beans, purple eyebrow beans, fresh mustard tuber, and "doll vegetable" that looks like a head covered with cabbage sprouts and belongs to the same mustard family as bok choy.

Local culture discovery

As a customer, I enjoy the markets' colourful displays, the sellers' shouting of prices and their interactions with their clients. Walking through markets can also teach us a lot about locals' beliefs and culture, and show us what locals eat.

For example, before Chinese New Year white turnips are everywhere and Napa cabbages are hung with red raffia all over the metal bars, making nice garlands above the stalls. This is also time when you can see heaps of pomelo leaves. Believers of Chinese old traditions will use them to rinse their body on Chinese New Year's Eve as it is said to be able to protect them from evil spirits. Greengrocers are stocked with waxed pork belly and sausages, some with a delicious rose-wine flavour, for making turnip cakes. Other stalls sell sweets, nuts and crystallised fruit as well as ready-made turnip and year cakes. In France, oysters, oranges, pineapples, walnuts, holly and mistletoes are the signs of the end-of-year festivities.

During the Mid-Autumn Festival which falls on the 15th

day of the 8th month of the lunar calendar, persimmons and pomelos are in season. Locals like to eat the fruit because their Cantonese pronunciations sound auspicious and are supposed to bring good fortune and symbolise union. Boiled taro and water caltrop, also called "bat nut" due to its resemblance to the winged mammal, are enjoyed as snacks during the festival. The former has a soft texture while the latter has a crumbly consistency. This is also time of the year when you see heaps of hairy crabs at Shanghainese greengrocers.

If you talk about food and recipes with locals, you might discover ingredients that are not used in Western countries. Such is the case for lye water. The alkaline solution gives noodles a yellowish colour and springiness to their texture. A few drops of the liquid are also added in the mooncake doughs to make their skin yellowish.

In France, when Christmas approaches, market stalls sell traditional holiday foods such as scallops, snails, cakes and fruit as well as plants to decorate homes. Scallops are the best in December and fishmongers offer both the molluscs raw in their shells and ready-cooked.

Seasonal sellers come to sell oysters and the sale is brisk as French people are big oyster lovers and like to eat them to celebrate the end of the year. The bivalves are best during the months that end with the letter "R" in French (from September to April). You can also enjoy freshly shucked oysters from the Atlantic Ocean with a glass of crisp Chablis at some markets.

Believers of Chinese old traditions use pomelo leaves to rinse their body on Chinese New Year's Eve as it is said to be able to protect them from evil spirits.

May this bring you good fortune.

Superstitious people hang mistletoe in their home to welcome the New Year as it is supposed to bring good luck to the household and ward off evils.

Greengrocers have crates full of the festival's favourite fruit: oranges, mandarins and pineapples. Pastry cooks sell traditional chocolate, chestnut or candied fruit and cream Yule log cakes (just like Ambassador's Cake). Butchers who sell ready-cooked dishes offer escargots with parsley, garlic and butter sauce ready to be heated up. Poultry farmers' stalls are loaded with geese as well as turkeys and capons (castrated cockerel) stuffed with chestnuts. Florists sell poinsettia, the most popular Christmas decorations all around the world as well as holly and mistletoe branches cut in the wood by farmers. At the Vienne market, you can also find walnuts from the Dauphiné region branches. In the past, sellers used to give the pearly white and red berries plants free to their regular customers. The French tradition is to hang mistletoe from ceilings to welcome the New Year so as to bring good luck to the household and ward off evils. Doesn't it sound similar to the pomelo leaves belief? Chinese people are not the only ones being superstitious!

Better service

I like to support market stalls for their personal touch. Shoppers, particularly elderlies, like markets for their convenience. They can just ask the vendors for what they want and they will then be served.

In France, vendors like talking about their products, giving recipes and, as relationships between clients and vendors develop over the years, asking about your family. Some people might think that it is just out of politeness and good for their business, but it is also very genuine and sincere. Vendors are usually kind and genuine, not fake kindness. Sellers know the importance of remembering customers' preferences. For example, in France, some clients like to have their pumpkin cut into sections because they find it hard to do it themselves and some do not want the carrot tops because they do not eat them.

In Hong Kong, most sellers are generally very kind too, though they take less time to serve each client. Like in France, vendors remember the preferences of their regular clients. For example, they will cut a long silk gourd into two so that it will not accidentally break during the clients' shopping and fall onto the ground. The stall owners on Argyle Street where I discovered so many unusual veggies have always been very kind to me. The middle-aged man and the elderly lady (I supposed mum and son) had never shown any sign of impatience or annoyance when I asked them the names of the vegetables, how to write them in Chinese and how to cook them.

I also like the service provided by the beef butcher stall at Tai Po Hui market that is manned by three women. Among them is the lady boss whom you would recognise straight away as she is the one with the dominant voice addressing customers in a confident way, always attentive and passionate. Her stall is always busy and closes very early in the afternoon. As she knows that I never come early, she suggests me phoning her if I want to order in advance. Then I will not get disappointed. How very thoughtful of her!

The stall where I buy most vegetables is in the main street near Tai Po Hui indoor government-run market. The shop is very old and full of boxes at the back. I like the graffiti-like on the wall behind it. The lady stallholder does not talk much, but is very kind and always smiles. Her husband, on his day off from work, usually sits on the side. Her older brother, next to her, sells regional fruits such as bananas, Chinese pears, green plums, etc. I am a regular customer and I know she will not give me bad veggies. Furthermore, in addition to the usual spring onions, she always gives me a bunch of coriander. She also advises me what is best to buy on that particular day and when I run out of ideas – deciding what to eat and setting a menu is the daily peeve of many of us – she gives me recipes. Clients next to me sometimes join in the conversation and give me ideas too.

Most of the times sellers are very kind and take time to explain to me how to cook or store this and that. For example, when I first bought bamboo shoots at a stall at Tai Po Hui market, the vendor explained to me that I needed to cut off the tips as those were too bitter to eat. She proposed to help me peel off the husks as she could do it in no time with her sharp tools. But before doing it, she asked me if I was to going to cook it on the same day; if not it was better not to remove the husks and she recommended wrapping it in newspaper and storing in a cool place until the following day. This kind of service is not available at supermarkets. I much prefer hearing tips from an experienced seller rather than on Internet.

Later when I went back to the same stall to buy bean curds, I noticed that the shoots looked different. I asked the lady vendor why they were much slender than before. This is how I learnt that from May to mid-August she sold a type called "horse hoof" due to its resemblance to the animal foot; from mid-August to January, the winter type; and from March to end of April, the spring type. The winter and the spring bamboo shoots were from China, but the horse hoof ones from Taiwan. Bamboo shoots are usually braised with pork but you can also pickle them. The horse hoof variety is good for stir-fry and can also be enjoyed raw in salad, as its flesh is very tender.

Fresh winter and spring shoots need to be parboiled before being braised so as to remove a somewhat poisonous substance. The horse hoof type does not have this "acid" body, so you only need to blanch it for a few minutes before stir-frying it. If you choose to eat it raw (for example shredded in a salad), there is no need to blanch it but just remember to discard the pointed bitter end.

Another day I asked the same vendor a recipe for edamame beans. She suggested stir-frying them with chopped pickled mustard tubers and dried bean-curds to make a complete and nutritious dish. At the same place, I discovered fresh lily bulbs and rice wild shoots. As before, the lady vendor taught me how to cook them.

I recall another lady vendor who gave me a variant of the winter melon soup. She told me to replace dried Chinese mushrooms and dried shrimps with dried lotus seeds, Chinese yam and fox nuts. I was not sure what the third item was and for sure I did not have any at home. She was very kind and proposed to accompany me to buy it. I told her that if I knew how to pronounce it in Cantonese I could manage myself, and asked her to repeat the name again. Then when I got the right intonation, I went to buy fox nuts for my soup. However, the vendor at this stall was not pleasant and seemed annoyed when I asked if I could open the prepacked fox nuts and check. As I suspected, something was wrong and I went back to the first store where I had bought the gourd to ask the lady for her opinion. She sniffed and inspected the nuts inside the plastic bag, her look showing that she did not feel completely satisfied. She said that the nuts were a bit too old but edible. She did not criticise the vendor at all, but just said that I should have gone to another stall to find a better quality.

One might expect sellers to be all friendly and welcoming, but it is not always the case, either in France or Hong Kong. While most of them are not exactly friendly, all of them are smiley. Building relationships with vendors is important if we want to get good produce and good weight.

Being a loyal customer is rewarding and sellers will never give you bad food.

Sellers usually give a few sprigs of spring onions to their clients.

Remember to cut the tip, and if you don't cook it today, wrap it in newspaper to preserve its freshness.

Kind sellers take time to give me cooking tips.

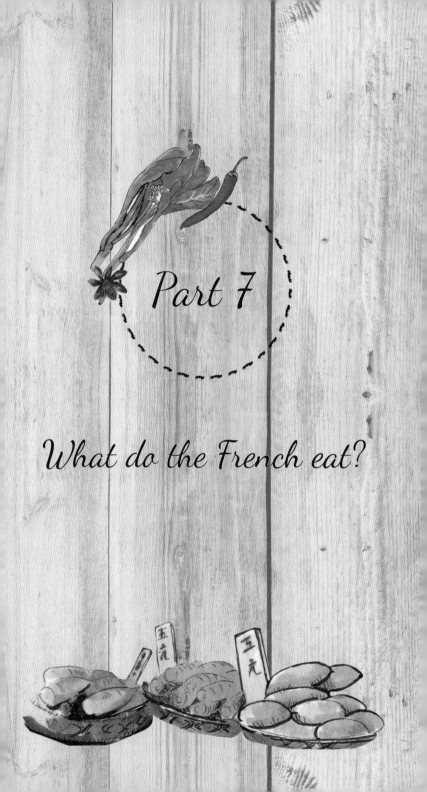

Part 7

What do the French eat?

Dishes

Eating is a pleasure. It is said that the French live to eat when most people eat to live and like to share meals. The same philosophy is valid with Hong Kong people who also associate food with life and health and are very much concerned with the medicinal properties of food.

The French like to take time with their meals and it is not uncommon for them to spend 3-4 hours around the dining table at Sunday lunches when celebrating holidays with family members. These lunches are usually held at home. In comparison, when celebrating festivals, people in Hong Kong meet for dinner rather than lunch, at home or outside.

Do the French eat foie gras and escargots every day? Do they always have rich sauces? Do they always have meals that last for ages? No, no and no. It would be the same as believing that all Chinese eat bird's nest, shark's fin, cordyceps, sea cucumber and snake soup each day. Of course they don't. In fact, most families cook simple dishes, such as the traditional steak frites, green salads, mashed potatoes and pasta, and buy sandwiches and ready-to-eat pizza, just to name a few. Traditional and hearty French dishes such as coq au vin (chicken stewed with red wine), boeuf bourguignon (a casserole of beef, vegetables, herbs, etc, cooked in red wine), pot-au-feu (simple boiled meal with roots and vegetables cooked in a very tasty broth) or potée (pork stew) need more time to prepare and are enjoyed at big family meals.

In the days of kings, French haute cuisine was famous for its multiple-course meals, large portions, centrepieces (dishes meant to impress) and sauces. Today new cuisine, often influenced by regional dishes, consists of smaller portions and focuses on high-quality ingredients.

Some dishes that I used to have when I was small and were common at Sunday and holiday meals, such as eggs and poached pike in aspic, Russian salad, macédoine (diced mixed vegetables), now go out of fashion.

Tricky sauces such as the hollandaise with egg-yolk, butter and creamy sauces are reserved for Sunday family lunches. Béchamel and tomato sauce are classics, easier to make and digest than cream-based sauces.

Breakfast

This is the lightest meal of the day. Contrary to Chinese people who like to start their day with a heavy meal and eat dim-sums, noodles or congee, French breakfast consists of a few toasts with jam or butter (or both!) or croissants that they like to dip in their coffee or tea.

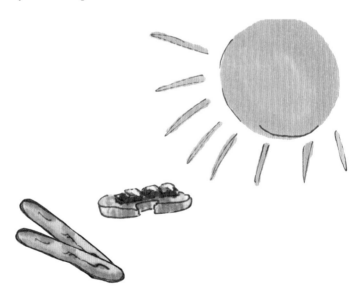

Lunch

Lunch used to be the biggest meal of the day when all family members came back home to eat. This style was common for farmers and factory workers who needed a hearty meal in the middle of the day. Today dinner is the biggest meal of the day for most families, as most people do not have time to go home for lunch.

In my family, we always had green lettuce salad as starter. This was followed by meat, or fish on Friday, vegetables, cheese (always after the main course), and a dessert or a piece of fruit. My mum always made sure that we had a balanced diet. Sometimes meat was replaced by an egg-based dish like quiche Lorraine or quenelles, which are dumplings shaped into sausages and poached. My mum served her homemade dumplings in a tomato and mushroom sauce. The way she made them differed from the Lyonnaise pike quenelles which are mousse-like, shaped between two spoons and served in creamy crayfish sauce. Her choux-pastry dumplings were softer.

Potato and pasta dishes were my favourites. At times, we had savoury rice dishes like risotto and pilaf, but definitely never steamed rice.

Dinner

In the evenings, dinner (or supper, the old-fashioned term) was simpler and consisted of a salad in summer and a potato and leek soup in winter, plus leftovers from lunch and a piece of fruit. If the leftovers were not enough, my mum would prepare potato fritters or an omelette.

Dinner is at around 8:00 pm whereas in Hong Kong people start to eat at 7:00 pm.

Desserts

Crepes, waffles and semolina cakes complemented our meal. They contained milk and eggs, and therefore were important for our growth and not regarded as bad foods. I remember the rice pudding, a dessert with rice and milk, quite different from the Chinese traditional snack made with rice flour and water. The best version of a rice or semolina cake that my mum made was when she added raisins and vanilla essence and served it with mulled wine spread on it. As if this was not sweet enough, my dad, who had a big sweet tooth, liked to top the dessert with a spoonful of homemade jam. Warm wine with spices is usually used to poach pears in another traditional Lyonnaise and Burgundy recipe we enjoyed in winter.

Tea-time or goûter

Snacks are important to French kids, and a snack and tea-time are both called "goûter." The verb "goûter" also means to enjoy or taste something for the first time.

I remember having gingerbread cake for my morning school snacks. I loved the honey and spicy flavours of "pain d'épices" that my mum ordered from my dad's factory work council. I recall when my dad came back home once and lamented about the quality of the cake my mum had given him for his morning shift snack. My mum then looked at the expiry date on the wrapping left in the tin and realised the cake was indeed very old. But the amusing thing is: my dad had such a sweet tooth that even the hardness of the cake did not deter him from eating it all!

After my dad told my mum that the gingerbread she gave him was quite hard...

She looked at the expiry date on the wrapping and realised the cake was indeed very old.

Another snack my mum bought from the factory work council was milk chocolate bars with hazelnut chips wrapped in an orange-coloured paper. I liked it very much and I regret that we can't find them at supermarkets anymore.

For our afternoon snacks on return from school, we had a humble toast with homemade jam or a slice of bread with chocolate squares or a fruit jelly bar. Today bread with chocolate squares is no longer a favourite after-school snack. Kids much prefer to have pre-packed fancy "goûter" than a simple slice of bread. At times, we had French toast made with leftover bread (read sub-chapter "French toast" in chapter Bread).

When my mum invited relatives or friends for tea, I could enjoy LU biscuits, named after the brand name and commonly called "Petit Beurre" or small butter that she offered to her guests. The famous dry cake with its 24 indents was invented in 1886.

On Wednesdays, as there was no school, my siblings and I took turns to make a cake. We selected recipes in a book designed for children, a promotional gift given out by a renowned plastic ware company. Of course, the cake-making process required the use of its own plastic measuring tools.

In Hong Kong, back in those years when I was still a primary school student in France, my (future) husband who was a secondary school student did not bring any food to school. But on weekends he would enjoy street snacks such as egg-puff waffles, rice pudding or curry fish balls. Today, kids in Hong Kong like crispy rice crackers, instant noodles that are eatable without any prior cooking, as well as savoury and sweet biscuits: sticks, cute koala-shaped or tubular-shaped biscuits filled with chocolate. I always wonder why the company making the latter had chosen to remind us of our digestive organ and given it a name with almost the same spelling.

Summer food: frogs and little fish

How often do the "froggies", as the English call French people, eat frog's legs? Not that often. The amphibian used to be considered as a delicacy in the south-east of France and they used to be caught in ponds in the Dombes area, north of Lyon. Today most of the frogs are imported from abroad, mainly from Vietnam, and you can buy frozen ready-to-cook ones at supermarkets. Frog meat does not have much taste itself and all is in the chopped parsley and garlic seasoning. If I say to Hong Kong people that I eat frog meat, they are not shocked because they, themselves, make clay pot rice with them. But the difference is that you can find live frogs at Hong Kong wet markets. You can even see the poor squirming batrachians being cut up in front of you. The scene is even crueller than seeing fish being gutted. Is it because the amphibians have legs?

In France, the summer speciality of open-air cafes and restaurants near large rivers is deep fried tiny silver-skinned fish. They are served with a tartar sauce and lemon wedges, and best accompanied with a simple green lettuce. In Lyon, "friture", the name of the dish, is made with bleaks that are usually caught in the Saône river, while along the Atlantic coast, it is made with smelt, a seawater fish. In the south of France, the dish is prepared with jol, which lives either in seawater or freshwater. You can also make friture at home with varieties of little fish that you find frozen at supermarkets. Another alternative is to go fishing and prepare your own catch.

I recall that my mum would deep-fry the bleaks or pan-fry the catfish that my dad had caught. He used to go fishing in the Rhône's arm, further back from the river bed. I remember when my dad would prepare his gears for the outing: fishing rods, buckets, maggots that he had coloured in red to better attract their prey and stored in sawdust, without forgetting the small folding chairs indispensable for the long hours during which he waited for the fish to bite. It was a hobby that he liked very much and the whole family went with him. We brought our picnic and stayed the full day near the river.

Later when I was older, my dad went fishing with his colleagues in a private pond owned by the factory they worked for. The pond was filled with carps and other common freshwater species, one quarter of them catfish. In addition to a national fishing licence, they needed a fishing card for that particular pond. The permit could be valid for a day, a week or a year. My husband and son had the opportunity to go with him a few times, his permit allowing him to bring guests.

In Hong Kong, you can see people fishing everywhere where there is water, even in reservoirs. I often see people fishing on both sides of the harbour, near the piers, either in Tsim Sha Tsui or Central, or the outlying islands. The amateur anglers do not seem concerned about the quantity of fish that they catch, but, like my dad, mostly enjoy the process of fishing.

Entertaining at home

The French like to share meals and invite relatives and friends to eat at their home. It is relatively easier for the French hostess to entertain than a Chinese hostess, as a French menu consists of 3 to 4 courses only. Chinese menus are more complicated and have to offer more varieties of food (both meat and fish, a soup and a starter, in addition to vegetables, etc.).

These are the two types of foods for entertaining at home:
- Food for families' reunions (Holiday food), and
- Food that requires less preparation or / and the participation of the guests (Convivial food).

Holiday food

Just like Chinese people, French people respect festivals and traditions. France has a lot of Christian festivals and the long hours of food preparation before Christmas or other Christian ceremonies, which allow family members to bond. For example, my dad, my siblings and I used to help to peel chestnuts for the Christmas log, crack walnuts for cakes or dress the table. My dad's additional job was to take care of the wine and aperitif, and shuck oysters – this required time, skill and attention so as not to cut one's hands.

Besides Christmas and Easter, the First and Solemn Communions, the two religious rites of passage for children and teens, are times for families to gather and share meals together. On these occasions, meals can last for three hours!

Foie gras, escargots and oysters are common food for the end-of-the-year festivities. In the 1970s, smoked salmon (not a French product) was expensive and we had it at Christmas only. This is not the case anymore today. Today many foods are being produced in large quantity and hence cheaper. Similarly, during the days when my parents were growing up, they did not eat meat every day but today it is the norm.

Escargots are considered a delicacy and, like frog's legs, their seasoning is the most important. However, if Hong Kong people don't eat gastropods, they make soups with different types of reptiles. I can't say that I love snake soup, but I don't dislike it either. The restaurant-made type tastes much better than the tinned version that my husband (my boyfriend at that time) made me try when we were students. I still recall the first time when he made me try it at the university residence. We reheated the soup on the portable electric hot plate and enjoyed our meal sitting on the bedroom floor.

On Epiphany day, a religious feast, it is customary to eat King's Cake. The lucky person who gets the trinket which is hidden in the cake will be crowned King or Queen. The small charm can represent the heads of royal family, but also animals or Christmas crib figures that are either made with porcelain or most often plastic. In Lyon, the traditional King's Cake is a puff pastry pie filled with frangipane, but you can also find ring-shaped cakes made of brioche pastry.

Candlemas or Crepe Day falls on February 2 each year. My siblings and I liked this Christian festival for the opportunity that it gave us to eat delicious homemade pancakes. My mum told us when we were small that housewives who believed that crepes protected their household from bad luck would flip one to their cupboard top each year on that day. In fact, one of our distant relatives used to flip pancakes while holding a coin in her hand to bring fortune to her household. I was sceptical on how they succeeded in throwing a crepe from the frying pan straight onto their wardrobe. I never had the curiosity to check by throwing one myself, even if there were any left rotten at home because my mum was not superstitious.

A superstitious housewife is flipping a pancake to her cupboard, believing that crepes will bring her good luck.

On the last day before Lent, a religious period when Christians fast, particularly on Ash Wednesday, the day when the fasting period starts, it is customary to eat sweet fritters. My mum made "bugnes" as they are called in the south-east of France. She made lots of them and invited relatives and friends to eat them, similar to the Chinese who make lots of turnip cakes at Chinese New Year. My siblings and I helped to roll the dough, cut it into strips of 10 cm x 4 cm with a pastry wheel cutter with a wavy edge and made an incision in each centre. My mum was the one to deep-fry the dough and as soon as the fritters came out of the oil bath, we sprinkled the piping hot fritters with confectioner's sugar. The thin pastry was brittle and we had to handle the doughnuts with care when arranging them in a large plate. A delicious odour of cooking oil and orange blossom water wafted in the whole house for the rest of the day and the following days!

At Easter, we had lamb which is a symbol of spring and new life. The traditional leg of lamb with flageolet beans or potatoes is still enjoyed at Easter, but the practice is fading away because now you can get lamb all year long coming from New Zealand. But one thing I did not like much at this festival was to eat lamb leg on Easter Sunday. I did not want to be reminded that the meat came from the baby lamb we had raised. We did not have a farm, so why did we end up with a ewe? It happened that one of my dad's colleagues was selling his farm animals and had convinced my dad to buy his sheep (at a very reasonable price) to clean the field next to our house which was left idle. This plot of land did not belong to my dad, but the landlord had agreed to let it to my dad for free. From time to time my siblings and I liked to watch her grazing and she became our pet. My dad even built a barn for our ewe. However, one day I heard my parents talking about bringing our ewe to mate and that she would have twins. Wow! Yes, this breed indeed carried twins. My siblings and I were very excited at the idea of having two lovely lambs. During the first week after their birth, we fed them with a little glass bottle filled with powdered milk. As soon as the rubber teats were inserted into their mouths, they sucked greedily. What a voracious appetite that they had! When they were about 2-3 weeks old, strong enough but not too heavy yet, my brother liked to carry them on his back and stroll around the field. The walk did not last long as the young animals did not appreciate much having their legs in the air. However, we slowly came to realise that we could not keep three sheep and the babies would eventually end up on our plate. My dad did not know nor did he have the guts to slaughter the lambs and had to ask my mum's uncle to do it for him. The reproduction and breeding processes were repeated for three consecutive years before my parents decided to stop, as it had become too painful for my dad to slaughter the lambs after having taken care of them. Lambs were sweeter than rabbits and hens.

I did not want to be reminded that the meat came from the baby lamb we had raised.

Chocolate eggs, sometimes huge ones filled with mini sugar eggs, and chocolate desserts remain the most popular Easter emblematic foods.

I recall Easter Sunday when my siblings and I rushed to the garden before even having our breakfast to hunt for the eggs that Easter bells had hidden in flowerpots, at the foot of a tree or behind the bench foot on their way back to Rome. In fact, my mum had boiled the chicken eggs with onion skins or beet juice to give them a nice copper or pink tint respectively and it was my dad who concealed them in the garden.

On Easter Sunday, my siblings and I rushed to the garden to collect Easter eggs.

Convivial food

Families in France cannot afford to have full-time domestic helpers like in Hong Kong and very often it is the wife (and mother) who prepares food, even if both spouses work full-time.

Thus, French ladies like to organise what is called a buffet dinner called "apéritif dînatoire." The potluck meal is ideal for hosts who do not want to cook a full meal on their own. It is often a delight for the eyes with lots of finger foods presented either in verrines (food presented in shot glasses), on toasts and rolls. Invitees like to blow their friends away by showing new recipes and combination of ingredients! During the summer days, the entire meal can be cold. This chummy and trendy way of entertaining is kind of new.

When it is getting colder, French people eat richer and more filling dishes that include cheese, potatoes, bacon and cold cuts and this is the time to make sauerkraut and onion soup. Single-course dishes such as raclette, Savoyard fondue, Bourguignonne fondue or pierrade (meat cooked on a heated stone) that require guests to participate in the making of their own food, similar to the Chinese hotpots, are also enjoyed.

Another convivial and single-course dish that I am thinking of is "farcement". One of our friends made it for us at the students' residence when my (future) husband and I were studying in Paris. This dish, a speciality from the Savoie Region where he came from, is made with diced salted pork, grated potatoes and Agen prunes mixed with eggs, crème fraîche and seasoning. The mixture is poured into a specific baking tin coated with smoked pork belly strips and then cooked in a bain-marie. The Chinese basin dish or "pun choy or pun choi" which has layers of ingredients such as seafood, mushrooms, roasted pork bellies, pig skin, bean curds, and vegetables reminds me of the filling Savoyard dish.

Charcuterie

Natives of Lyon and its vicinity are known for loving pork meat and charcuterie. Unfortunately, there is no such thing as charcuterie in Hong Kong. Waxed sausages and braised soya meat or offal (lo sui) are the closest foods to French charcuterie.

Lyon is famous for its "bouchons" or taverns serving chitterling sausages, pork trotters or warm Lyon sausages with potato salad. "Bouchon" means a cork or plug, like the one we use for a wine bottle, but it also means blockage or even traffic jam.

There is a saying in French "tout est bon dans le cochon", meaning that everything in the pig has its use, except the bile. "Bon" and "cochon" mean "good" and "pig" respectively in French, and rhyme. Even the less popular cuts are nicely deboned and ready for making a delicious dish. Neither do Chinese people waste any part of the animal, but lower cuts and offal are not as nicely prepared as French butchers do and as a result not very attractive.

Offal

Both in France and in Hong Kong, every part of the pig is cooked and nothing is wasted. In France, cow's testicles and udder are usually coated with breadcrumbs and pan-fried. Udder meat is said to be tender but rather bland.

I have never heard that French people eat bull's penis (called "spring pocket" in Cantonese), or cow's ovaries or vulva. I saw on Internet that there is a restaurant in Yuen Long that serves all of these, in case you want to try! And if you are brave enough, I am sure you can order the organs at your butcher. I, myself, have not tried cow's ovaries, but frog's ovaries in soup as a recovery food after the birth of my son. Once I had vermicelli soup with bull's penis ("whip" in Cantonese) at a small eatery in Tai Po and it tasted like tendon.

Another weird offal that is sold in Hong Kong is pig's roof of the mouth (called sky-stairs or a stairway to heaven). Usually the long white ribbed sliver is sold attached to the pig's tongue, but you can buy a few for your hotpot. A plate of about 10 pieces will make a nice stew. It is said to be crispy and tasty. I have yet to try it!

In France, tripe, raw and some cooked, are not only sold by butchers but also specialised tripe merchants. In Hong Kong, parts of fresh offal are sold by butchers; blanched ones, like tripe and intestines, by tofu sellers; and marinated ones by specialised shops selling "lo-sui".

France has a long tradition of eating pork. In the past, farmers used to raise a few hogs for their own consumption and slaughtered them when they were 2-years-old, usually in March and November. When the pigs were slaughtered, it was customary for farmers to offer to their neighbours a plate of freshly cooked blood pudding surrounded with parts of pig's offal which were eaten in fricassee, which means braised in a heavy cast-iron skillet or pan-fried. Heart and lungs were the first parts to be eaten, followed by the spleen which was roasted. Later during the week, liver and kidney would be pan-fried and served in a thick sauce. Pork rind and fatback would then be rendered into lard that was used for cooking. Nothing was wasted! Nowadays lard is used for making crispbread, biscuits and in baking products (pie crust, shortcrust pastry, etc.). In Hong Kong, pork white fat is also sold to bakeries as well as dim sum restaurants to make buns, siu-mai and other dumplings.

My mum used to prepare "fressure d'agneau" or lamb's pluck (lungs, liver and heart) as per my paternal grand-mother's recipe, that is, cut in pieces, sautéed and served with chopped parsley and garlic. Sometimes she added a spleen and sweetbread, coated the offal with flour and stewed them with red wine.

I recall that one of my relatives used to buy cow's lungs and sometimes heart or spleen to feed her house cat. Our cat was free to go outside and could catch mice for his meals, so we did not need to buy extra proteins for him. Nowadays industrial pet food is the preferred choice of pet owners.

Each year, sport clubs and associations near Vienne raise funds by selling pig's blood sausages. The pork intestine is filled with pork fat, cream, herbs and seasoning. The event is held on a winter Sunday under a marquee or inside a community centre. On that day, experienced villagers prepare "boudin" in the club premises. The sausages are boiled in large iron caldrons outdoors. Some events are so popular that people from other neighbouring communes come to buy the delicacy and support the local associations. They have to make sure that they arrive early if they don't want to return home empty-handed. I recall that once I went late in the morning and was told that everything had been sold out by 10:30 am. Many people take the opportunity to enjoy a glass of white wine with their friends while tasting free bits of the dark sausages at the refreshment area before going home.

In winter, you can also buy homemade blood sausages at the butchers' or stalls specialised in charcuterie.

Potatoes

The French eat a lot of potatoes. All kids love spuds, as they call them. Who does not like French fries or "frites" or jacket potatoes? The latter is called "dressing-gown potatoes" in French, which is funnier than the English name. I loved my mum's crunchy potato fritters called "doormats", another name that made me burst out laughing when I was small: "ha ha ha! We are going to eat a doormat!" The modest fritters will become a full meal when served with bacon, mushrooms or salmon, or even with more luxurious ingredients such as truffles or foie gras.

In primary school, I learnt that French people did not initially like the tuber that originated from South America. The humble vegetable was then promoted to fight hunger during the French Revolution and made popular by an apothecary, Mr Parmentier, as potatoes were resistant to cold and easier to store than wheat. To convince Louis XVI of their benefits, Mr Parmentier made him try "mashed potato and minced beef", a dish that was later called after him and known today as "Hachis Parmentier" or the

Shepherd Pie. Thereafter potatoes have been prepared in many different ways and each region has its own potato dish specialities.

Most potato dishes are filling and most of them are best enjoyed during the winter days like "Tartiflette", a dish with Reblochon cheese, lardons and onions (from the Alps) or the traditional "Gratin Dauphinois" (a baked dish which consists of layers of potato slices covered with cream) from the Dauphiné area (close to the Alpes region). My mum's gratin differed from the original version. She used to replace cream with milk, which was economical and healthier, and added only some bits of butter on top as well as grated nutmeg. She also made the lighter Lyonnaise version called "pommes de terre boulangère" in which chicken broth replaced milk, and had onion and a bouquet garni to add flavour.

Mashed potatoes are also a big favourite of kids. There was a dried version that you bought in packs at supermarkets, but once you have tried the real dish made with fresh potatoes, with bits of butter and a pinch of freshly grated nutmeg, it was difficult to like the "fake" version we had at the school canteen. Even if you substitute milk for water to rehydrate the dried potatoes flakes, it is not as tasty as fresh potatoes.

I also recall the trend of Duchess potatoes, which had a similar soft melt-in-your-mouth texture as potato gnocchi that my paternal grandmother used to make. I can't recall my grand mum's cooking skills as she was quite old when

I was born but she had passed on her recipe to my mum. My dad was always in charge of pounding our home-grown basil leaves with garlic by hand, with a wooden mortar and pestle so as to release their full flavours and make a creamy pesto sauce that is so perfect to accompany the dumplings.

My friend and her husband have been growing organic vegetables and fruit for the past 30 years and, among them, about 15 varieties of potatoes (which is only a few from the existing 380 types), some with red skin, others with blue-purple flesh, but all with beautiful and feminine names such as Anais, Amandine, etc. None of these species can be found at Hong Kong wet markets. My friend encourages her clients to try different kinds and gives them recipes so that they can better appreciate the characteristics of each variety. Flaky-textured tubers are best baked or mashed while waxy-textured ones best roasted. One of her recipes I like best is "Bacon-Wrapped Potato Bundles" which consists (as per its name) of sautéed potato slices that are wrapped in bacon and baked. She recommends to use Bintjes or Monalisa, which have firm flesh and to serve them with green beans and a roasted guinea fowl.

We were a family of five and each winter we consumed more than 100 kg of potatoes. The potato is a staple food and as mentioned above my mum made a potato and leek soup in winter and also cooked potato dishes a few times a week.

I can still remember fondly the times when I went with

my parents to pick up potatoes in a farm owned by distant relatives.

Each year at the end of summer our expedition started. The farm was in a village, about 45 minutes away from our home. We had to cross an area called "Cold Lands" or "Hilly Lands" where the soil was poorer and the climate harsher, windier and colder than in the Rhône valley where we lived. My mum drove the Citroen 2CV that was well suited for the purpose of our trip, i.e. to carry back the potatoes from the farm. This car, today a French icon and France's most famous car, was very practical with its removable rear seat that allowed to carry bulky things in the boot. It was actually designed to carry 50 kg of potatoes, two farmers and a barrel of wine! In our case, the two passengers were my mum and my granddad and my dad took his mother-in-law, my brother and me in his R10.

Each year at the end of summer our expedition started.

We started our potato collection in the late afternoon to avoid the strong sun. The soil had already been turned and in the shallow furrows the potatoes were waiting to be harvested. The potato plants wilted quickly under the scorching sun. We picked the roots that had been pulled by the tractor's blades by hands and we unearthed any potatoes left uncovered in the soil, shaking each plant to make sure that no potatoes were left attached to its roots. We started our harvest by squatting, but as we grew tired we ended up kneeling down. In his painting "The Collect of Potatoes", Jules Bastien Lepage depicts this activity with acute realism!

We started our harvest by squatting, but as we grew tired we ended up kneeling down.

Within three hours we would be finished and the men would load our produce – more than 130 kg+ (about 100 kg for my parents plus 30 kg for my grandparents) – part in the 2CV and the remainder in the other car. It was quite exhausting! The price we paid for the potatoes was a good deal because we had participated in the harvest. The good potatoes were collected in baskets and any tubers that had been damaged by the blades were put aside. The latter would be used to feed pigs and poultry.

Our Citroen 2CV was well suited for the purpose of our trip, i.e. to carry back the potatoes from the farm.

Before we returned home, our relatives always insisted on having a bite to eat together. All foods came from the farm: smoked pork belly, saucisson, mushroom omelette, apples and walnuts, and the traditional tomme daubée served with boiled potatoes. The name of the dish could put off many as daubée means stank or scorned in French, but I assure you that it is misleading. It is originally from the Dauphiné region and is made with cottage cheese mixed with white wine or vinegar, oil, thick dairy cream, shallots and chives. The white and smooth texture resembled those of calf brains and the Lyons' middle class gave it the name of "Canuts brain" simply because the Canuts, the people working in Lyon's silk industry in the 19th century, could not afford to eat real calf brains such as pan-fried calf brain, the Lyonnaise delicacy.

After a hearty dinner, we returned home feeling satisfied with our day and enough provision for the forthcoming winter.

All foods came from the farm: saucisson, mushroom omelette, apples and walnuts, and the traditional tomme daubée served with boiled potatoes.

Potatoes are not popular in Chinese cooking and are mainly used in family dishes such as potato and tomato soup, stew with chicken wings, Portuguese-style chicken curry or patties with minced pork. I could only find one variety that was too sweet for my liking. Today market stalls carry the same variety that is either grown in Mainland China or Hong Kong, but supermarkets carry different kinds: some from Japan, others from Australia, the USA and even Lithuania.

School canteen food

The school canteen is an institution in France. Each school must provide meals to their students within its premises. Canteen provides a full meal to students that always includes a starter, a main dish, a cheese or dairy product and a fruit and / or dessert. School canteens not only provide a nutritious meal to students, but also have an educational and social role, particularly to the younger students. Primary school's students learn to try every food, not to waste and finish their plate. For many of them this is an opportunity to eat veggies as their parents come back late from work and have no time to prepare balanced meals in the evening. Making a pasta dish is easier but also avoids disputes at the dinner table as most children don't like to eat veggies.

I already mentioned in this book foods that we find at school canteens such as instant mashed potatoes and the laughing cow cheese that I considered fake and artificial. I also hated to eat spinach at the canteen. Unlike at home where my mum always used fresh vegetables, school canteens mainly used canned vegetables for convenience. Canned spinach was chopped so finely that once mixed in a white sauce it had to be served with a ladle. The view of the dark green liquid was disgusting. Furthermore, it seems that we always had spinach the day after the school lawn had been cut and when we looked out the window, we could not help but think that the dish had been made with the grass!

During my primary schooling, I seldom ate at the school canteen and would have liked to go more often, just for the laughing cow processed cheese and the LU biscuits we were rewarded if we helped the staff canteen to dry the dishes. Later when I was in secondary school and had to eat at the canteen every day, I wished my parents lived closer so that I could return home for lunch.

Restaurants

Both in France and Hong Kong, food presentation is important and not only the taste but also the colours and odours are essential elements to any dishes. Both places like to use fresh produce and have a tradition of elaborated dishes that require a long preparation time. Hong Kong is famous for its dim sum culture, offering a large variety of food served in small portions, similarly to the Spanish tapas.

However, there are some differences in terms of pace, service efficiency, hygiene and manner to ask for the bill.

The French like to take time especially at weekends, be they lunch or dinner. Sit-down dinner or buffet for wedding or birthday celebrations is served at a much slower pace than Chinese style banquets, and people dance until the wee hours of the morning. In Hong Kong, people meet before the meal to chat, play mah-jong and take photos, and by 11:00 pm the feast is over.

In France, customers need to wait for a while before being given the menu and asked if they like a drink before eating. If you ask for water, you will be served a bottled water but if you ask for a carafe, tap water is free of charge. In Hong Kong, the service is speedier and drinks are served immediately after you are seated. People, particularly women, like to drink hot or warm water for health reason.

Some Hong Kong eateries, particularly dai-pai-dong (food stalls) and cha-chan-teng (Chinese style coffee shops) are far from being spotless, and hygiene obsessed customers are easily scared off because bins and piles of dirty plates and cutlery are often in their full view.

When it is time to get the restaurant bill, Hong Kong people make a hand gesture to indicate they want to pay. In France, you can't do that and you need to make extended eye contact with the waiter / waitress so that he / she understands you need something and come to you; then, you will ask him / her to bring you the bill.

Picnics

The French like to picnic, particularly in summer. Some picnics are planned a long time in advance, such as those held annually to gather with family, which is called "cousinade", or neighbours. When neighbourhood residents meet on that special occasion, they cordon off their street and set tables and chairs to enjoy a meal together. People living in blocks of flats use the block's entrance. I never joined this type of meeting as there was none in my parents' village when I was still living with them.

To have a picnic with a large group of people is a convenient, friendly and economical way to meet many people altogether. Nobody in particular has to worry about cooking and cleaning the dishes, unlike the traditional meals at home. Each family simply needs to bring some food to share. However, the dishes can be quite elaborate and people try to impress everyone with new recipes, bringing some changes from the traditional rice salad with tuna. As strange as it might sound, I have never made rice salad in my life because my husband does not like cold rice. Rice is the staple food of Chinese people and is eaten in many ways, but I have never had a savoury cold rice dish in Hong Kong.

I recall the picnics that my family had on our way to our summer vacation or day trip. Eating on a field or the edge of a forest away from the main road allowed us to stretch our legs and eat casually. Going to a restaurant with three young kids would have been too much hassle and costly. It was never easy to find a good place, away from the traffic but not too far from the main road, and not yet occupied by holidaymakers already having their lunch. Often my dad drove too fast and could not stop timely at the beautiful site that my mum had caught sight of, and we could feel some tension in the air. As time passed, we all started to get hungry and looked around helping to discover a suitable place where we could stretch our legs and fill our stomachs. Once a vacant spot was finally found, we stopped and my dad took the picnic materials from the car boot and we unfolded the blankets and the small folding chairs. My mum would spread a piece of red and white plaid tablecloth on the grass and unpack the food and utensils that she had prepared in a stylish picnic hamper. We had plastic plates and glasses that were reusable but stainless steel cutlery and linen napkins. We had the luxury of having a pepper grinder and a salt shaker, in case we would like to season our food. She usually made a niçoise salad which made a full dish, as it is made with tomatoes, hard-boiled eggs, tuna and anchovies. Rice salad which is kind of niçoise salad but with cold cooked rice was another common option. To complement our meal, we also had cold cuts: cooked ham or saucisson and cheese that we ate together with bread bought at the village bakery before taking to the road. And we finished our meal with a fruit bought earlier on the road from local producers, and my dad a homebrew coffee stored in a thermos.

I also recall the light and simple picnics that I had by the Ardèche[7] river when I went rafting with my parents and their friends during one of the prolonged weekends the French enjoy in May, that is when they take one or two extra days off between a public holiday and their usual rest-days. We used to go down the river in one of those former military inflatable rafts that had been sold to the public after World War II. We started our outing very early in the morning and stopped on our way to the starting point at a bakery to buy bread.

Our lunch was less elaborate than normal picnics due to the temperature and the limited space on the boat. We brought food that were easy to eat on the go such as whole tomatoes, hard-boiled eggs and fruit that we put in a large plastic box to prevent them from getting wet. We did not have space for an icebox, thus we could not bring any delicate food as our lunch had to stay a few hours in the confined environment before being consumed. No quiche, no salad and no cheese. Definitely not cheese! The later would have run and filled the other food with its fragrance.

---

[7] Ardèche department is less than 60 km south of Vienne (located in Isère department).

Some French picnics are simple and take less time to prepare, like those we do when travelling or making an outing such as fishing, picking up mushrooms, or just spending a day outdoors. And bread always plays an important part in picnics. Forgetting to bring bread to a picnic would be a mistake and this essential companion to cold cuts and cheese cannot be absent! Although people try to refrain themselves from eating bread because it is high in calories, some people, like me, find it difficult to go without it.

Having picnics in Hong Kong is not common because people prefer hot food to cold food. They consider hot food to be better for their health and it also makes them feel full. Thus, it is no surprise that barbecuing is one of the preferred social activities that people enjoy during autumn and winter when the weather is cooler and dryer. Hong Kong people usually buy barbecue food and tools on the day of their outing before heading for country parks where pits are set at their disposal.

Preparation is minimum. They buy pre-marinated meat, sausages, fish balls, seafood and chicken wings that they baste with honey that is bought specially for that purpose and comes with a brush. Each individual takes care of his or her overloaded two-prong fork until the food is perfectly cooked. Corn, mushrooms, sweet potatoes are wrapped up in foil and set aside on the grill to cook on their own. Kids like to roast marshmallows! Cleaning is efficient as metal mesh grills and forks can simply be disposed of in the nearest public rubbish bin!

As the Chinese socialise while cooking their food, the French prefer to enjoy food that has been prepared in advance and, like me, don't want to dirty their hands! We even bring blankets and folding chairs so that we can sit comfortably while picnicking.

Bread

Do we eat bread? Yes! …a lot!

A piece of bread might be a humble food, but it is a very important food in French people's diet and the French are very picky when it comes to bread. Each family has its own favourite bakery as the taste and quality of one baguette vary from another. The French like to eat fresh bread and buy the right portion so as to avoid having any leftovers. Nobody likes stale bread and it is possible to buy only half of a baguette.

I learnt from a young age not to waste food and finish everything that was on my plate, as well as any left piece of bread. If ever I commented that it was only a little morsel and not food waste, my mum would retort: "you have never endured war." I could not imagine how it was to go without food, but the mention of war sounded quite scary and I would not argue and hurried to finish the bit of bread.

Most people like to keep bread in the freezer as they fear of being short of their daily food. You can also buy baguettes in vending machines, in front of some bakeries or in small villages that do not have any bakery. You can also buy from these vending machines during lunch time, as bakeries are closed from 12:00 noon to 2:00 pm.

The traditional baguette is still the favourite of French people, although farmhouse and wholemeal breads are common alternatives. You thought France was a free economy? Rules have been governing bakers since the bread shortage in 1789 and bread prices were fixed until 1986. And until 2015, bakers used to be informed by the city's administrative authorities which week in July and August they could take day off. This creates a lack of fresh bread particularly in August, as most bakers prefer holidaying at that time.

We start to eat bread very early in our life: from 6-months-old, grandmas and mums give teething babies a crust of bread so they can chew on it. Later, adults need to "earn their crust", in other words to work. And we informally use the term "casser la croûte" or break a crust when we have a snack or eat a sandwich.

Bread is present at the three main meals of the day. Our traditional breakfast starts with toasts and bread is always present for lunch and dinner. Ah! Unlike in Hong Kong, the French don't eat butter with bread, except for their morning toasts.

When I came to Hong Kong, I learnt quickly to eat

without bread and soon liked rice all the same. I used chopsticks to shovel rice into my mouth and forgot about pushing bread to mop up the last of the sauce on my plate or load food onto my fork (which is acceptable for kids). I love bread, but I stopped eating baguette gradually since I have been living in Hong Kong because there was no French bakery close to my home and baguette could not be kept for a long time. I recall when my husband and I used to buy a loaf of bread on our way home after dining at my mother-in-law's place in 1987. I liked to rip pieces off the soft crumbs from the plastic bag to eat even when I was already full. This used to upset my husband, as he feared that people would think that he could not afford to feed his wife properly. For me, there was nothing bad about it. The French like to cut a chunk of bread with their fingers after getting out of the bakery to eat straight away. I have this habit too! The crust of fresh bread is so good, especially if it is still warm.

Talking about French habits, we also do something that sounds strange to foreigners, i.e. we carry bread under our arm and put it directly on the tablecloth and not on our plate. Some people may joke that we don't worry about hygiene, which is quite true. Actually, bakeries today put bread in a paper bag or wrap it partly in paper. Once bread has left the bakery, its crust is exposed to different environments: car seat, car rear deck, sideboard or kitchen unit. Some shoppers like my mum bring their bread bag to carry bread and protect it from being exposed to dirty places. My mum made her own fabric bag that is large enough to put a few baguettes in. My sister told me that she remembers when she used to ride to the bakery on her bike and carry bread on her bike rack. Once she did not tie it properly, the elastic cord got loose and the baguette fell on the street. When she realised that she had dropped the bread, she just returned to pick it up and brought it home without saying anything to anyone!

I recall our home's bread bin made of red and white braided plastic with a hinged lid and a handle. Baguette cabinets are still used today, although built-in versions are more common as well as baskets.

French like to cut a chunk of bread with their fingers after getting out of the bakery to eat straight away.

Once my sister did not tie the baguettes that she bought from the bakery properly on her bike and the baguettes fell onto the street when the elastic cord got loose.

The soft and warm chocolate tasted much better than the hard and cold squares. I had to wait for quite a while, but what a delicious reward!

At the annual boat jousting competition in our village, volunteers cooked sausages on a grill and served them in a baguette sandwich with mustard.

215

French toast

Although we never wasted bread, there were occasions when we did eat a bit less than usual and there was some leftovers. In that case, my mum who was thrifty would use the stale bread to make "pain perdu" which literally means lost bread. The dessert was nothing other than a humble version of what is called French toast in English, and consisted of slices of bread dipped into beaten eggs and milk, pan-fried in a buttered saucepan and topped with granulated sugar. The Hong Kong name is sai^1 do^1-si^2, the character sai^1 being the shorten form for France (faa^3-laan^4-sai^1) and do^1-si^2 meaning toast. This version is more luxurious and fattening, but all the same delicious. It resembles more like a deep-fried peanut butter sandwich and is served with a thick slice of butter and sugar syrup. Today people use fresh brioche to make French toasts.

Melted chocolate on bread

I was about 10 years old when my Mum had a varicose vein removed. During her convalescence, I was sent to spend a few days at one of my father's colleagues. The family of four had two teenage daughters and lived in a farm. The father worked on shift, thus allowing him to help his wife at the farm when he was off duty. Their kitchen floor had no tiles and always seemed dirty even after the mother had washed it clean. At times, there was some strange smell that I suspected coming from poultry droppings. Indeed, the birds were running free and entered the house whenever they had a chance to, looking for bread crumbs.

It was there where I learnt how to make a deluxe version of the chocolate and bread snack.

I cannot recall what I did in the morning, but remember very well my afternoon activities. After lunch, I brought the goats to graze in the fields with the younger daughter. We sat on the grass and I read a book or knitted. She was not talkative and busy flipping through women's magazines which I was not allowed to look at. What could a teenage girl talk about with a little girl? The elder daughter was often exempted from the task – to tell the truth she did not seem to appreciate the country life a lot.

About two hours later, we would return home, the herding dog running back and forth to keep the flock together and making sure that none of the agile creatures were left behind. Once back to the farm and the goats being safely kept in their barn, we went to cool down in the house. We were rewarded with a glass of lemonade, a big slice of country bread, not the baguette type at all, and one chocolate bar.

To my surprise, her daughter did not eat it straight away but went out of the house with her snack, asking me to follow her. She then placed the chocolate on top of the bread and sat the open-sandwich on a low wall that was moss free. I did the same and we waited for the sun to melt the chocolate. We waited for quite a while, but what a delicious reward it was! The soft and warm chocolate tasted much better than the hard and cold squares. The following days we did the same and each time I tried to find a better place, hoping to accelerate the process but all depended on the fierceness of the sun on that day. This was how we made our own chocolate spread. Not quite the same as the famous one with crunchy bits and the hazelnut flavour, but still a delicious and creamy one! I still remember the foal on the packaging illustrating the chocolate brand name. Each chocolate tablet had a picture of an animal that children liked to collect. Some parents were willing to buy the specific album in which the pictures could be kept in an organised way.

Bread with charcuterie

Bread is also enjoyed with cold cuts as mid-day snacks, particularly by countryside dwellers and manual workers who need hearty snacks to stand long working hours. This used to be the case of my grand-dad. My maternal grandfather was a postman and used to cycle no less than 40 km each day to deliver the mails to the three surrounding villages. He left his home very early to set off on his rounds and when the clock stroke nine, he would stop to refill his energy level with a slice of bread and smoked pork belly. Today postmen deliver mails by car and no longer need such robust snacks.

My grand-dad never missed his "casse-croûte (literally break-crust) even after his retirement and I was happy whenever I was on holiday at his home as he would offer me to try some of his snack. I recall him cutting bread and charcuterie with his "Opinel", a pocket-knife with a wooden handle and a metal ring to block the blade in open position that he liked to keep with him at all times.

Bread with cheese

Bread goes hand in hand with cheese.

Cheese has an important place in our meals. When I was small, I often heard adults say, "we always need to keep a small place for cheese", as it contains elements that are supposed to help neutralise the excess of gastric acid. The French will always make sure that they have enough bread for cheese, as no meal is complete without some cheese. It is true that nothing is as good as bread to accompany cheese. I recall how I feared I would miss cheese in Hong Kong and how happy I was when I saw in a Paris' Chinatown grocery something in a basin that looked like semi-soft tomme cheese. I shouted: "Chinese made cheese too!" But my joy was quickly dampened when my boyfriend (now my husband) explained to me that the white blocks were made with soya bean and called tofu or bean-curd. I did not immediately appreciate the Chinese cheese when I first tried it. I admit that I found it bland and it did not taste at all like unripened pressed cheese. However, later in Hong Kong I discovered a sauce made with preserved white bean curd when eating the "braised lamb in clay pot" that tasted like blue cheese. Since then, I always keep a jar of preserved white bean curd in my fridge to put in stir-fried water spinach to add sharpness to the leafy vegetable with hollow stems, and to spread on my homemade wholemeal no-knead bread as a substitute for cheese.

Sandwiches

The French eat less bread but more sandwiches. Sandwiches are the equivalent of wonton noodles in Hong Kong. Today there are plenty of sandwich fillings making it difficult to make one's choices, but a good-quality baguette with traditional ham and butter remains my favourite. Today in Hong Kong, you can find good-quality sandwiches too.

Another type of sandwich I liked but could not find in Hong Kong was the merguez sandwich. The spicy mutton or beef-based sausage originates from the North-African cuisine and reminded me of families' barbecues and sports events where the grilled sausages' aroma could be smelled from far away. Summer was the best time for sports associations to celebrate end-of-year activities to raise money or host sports events.

I particularly recall the annual boat jousting competition in our village where volunteers cooked spicy and non-spicy sausages on a grill and served them in a baguette sandwich with mustard.

Similar to dragon boat racing, boat jousting is a water sport performed with a musical background in a festive atmosphere. The ancient spectacular sport is popular in France. It was originally organised to entertain the kings and their courts and has been recognised as an official sport in 1980. A band plays on the riverside and its tunes vary to fit the fights. Whereas the dragon boats race forward to reach the finish line with the sound of a drum, in boat jousting two small boats hurry to reach their opponents with the sound of a brass band and two jousters (one on each boat) face each other trying to throw his / her adversary into the water.

The refreshment area was a good source of revenue as the scorching sun helped to draw people there to quench their thirst.

During my first years in Hong Kong, I missed the spicy sausage. When one day I found out that merguez could be bought at one of the supermarkets catering for foreigners, I rushed to buy a few. However, when I was enjoying them, I realised that I missed the festive environment more than the food itself. Similarly, the food I bring back from France does not taste the same when I eat it in Hong Kong.

Part 8

Do the French drink wine every day?

Drinking wine is a French tradition and an important cultural element in French cuisine. It goes hand in hand with festivals and celebrations. Chinese wine culture has also a long history, although most wines are made from grains.

Most people assume that all the French people drink wine every day. Is it true? French people drink to celebrate amongst friends in the weekend and some enjoy a daily glass of wine to accompany their meal. About 13% only drink every day and almost half of the population drink at least once a week.

Is it true that in France wine can be cheaper than a cup of coffee? People like to joke about the price of one glass of table wine being cheaper than one cup of espresso. It is true that a 10-cl glass of ordinary wine, like a Burgundy aligoté, costs 1 euro versus 1.20 euros for an espresso. This white wine is good for a simple aperitif or kir (mixed with blackcurrant liqueur) and the cheapest bottle costs as low as 6 euros, but not many people drink it pure as they prefer better wines. Hence, drinking wine has become more expensive than drinking a cuppa. A kir royal is made with Champagne.

Do children drink wine? It used to be common for children in their early teens to start drinking wine diluted with water at family dinners and holidays. It was not seen as either bad or good, but more of a tradition. Similarly, drinking alcohol at school canteen used to be legal and it was only from 1956 that it was forbidden for students aged

14 or below, and not before September 1980 for senior secondary students. Fortunately, we don't hear any more stories of parents adding drops of wine in their baby's bottle. Water is children's main drink at family meals and usually there are no fuzzy drinks on the table.

Do all French people have a wine cellar full of good bottles? They do not, but the majority keep wines at home and about one quarter have a wine refrigerator. They like to keep bottles because it is convenient to have some at home, and most of them drink it with their family or give them out as gifts. Only a few buy for investment.

I recall when I first went to a wedding banquet in Hong Kong and saw people mixing Coca-Cola with brandy. What a waste! The consumption of the golden liqueur has reduced drastically over the past 30 years, while that of wines has increased substantially. In France, strong alcohol consumption has also reduced due to the stringent laws against drunk-driving. The French are no longer taking liquor or "digestif" after their coffee, for fear of being caught and having their licence revoked.

Today many Hongkongers know about wine and wine making, and have visited French wineries. However, the wine cellars of the northern Rhône valley, the region where I came from are not as well-known as those of Bordeaux or Burgundy areas. There, traditional wines are produced and Syrah and Viognier grapevines are producing the two notorious appellations (AOC) Côte-Rôtie and Condrieu which are grown on the steep sloping areas close to my hometown.

Organic viticulture is growing in France. In 2016, 9% of vineyards produced organic wines, of which 1/3 in the Languedoc-Roussillon region, and one consumer out of 6 drank organic wine. (Source: Agence bio).

Is toasting an important aspect of a banquet or big dinner? It is. French people toast once at the beginning of the meal whereas Chinese people like to toast at the start of each dish.

Today many specialised retailed stores and online shops offer a wide choice of wines from all around the world. Wine clubs are very popular too and Hongkongers drink more wine than ever before. When I came to Hong Kong in 1986, the choice of wine at supermarkets was very limited. I recall the name of Mateus, the Portuguese semi-sparkling rosé in ovoid bottles, and Mouton-Cadet red Bordeaux. The latter was over-priced at HK$99. It costs about HK$170 today. I also recall the slogan "Le Beaujolais nouveau est arrivé!" or "The new Beaujolais has arrived" at supermarkets where the popular red light-bodied wine, fermented for a few weeks only, was released on its official date; i.e. each year on the 3rd Thursday of November.

Part 9

Different varieties and tastes

Tomatoes and carrots that I find in Hong Kong do not taste as sweet as in France. Produce growing in different soil and different climate do not have the same taste.

Back in 1986, I missed a simple green lettuce. When I was living with my parents, our lunch always started with a green leaf lettuce usually from our garden. I could not find the curly or broad-leaf French endives that I liked to eat with walnuts and Gruyère cheese, nor the mesclun (mixed green salad) that is simply delicious with mustard vinaigrette. Obviously, I could not find dandelions as those grow wild in fields. The plants are picked in spring when they are young and not too bitter. They taste delicious with anchovies and soft-boiled eggs or with sautéed poultry liver or gizzard.

There were about 20 varieties of lettuce commonly grown in France, but in Hong Kong, I could only find the Iceberg type (the closest type to Batavia lettuce) and the Chinese lettuce with its curly or smooth-edged leaves and thinner texture. The crisp iceberg leaves were stir-fried or used raw to wrap minced meat and other ingredients while Chinese lettuce was also stir-fried or added in congee, stews or soups. The wilted lettuce leaves reminded me of sweet peas "à la française" served at the school canteen, which I used to hate.

I also missed the leek and potato soup my mum made in winter. The Chinese leeks or chives are slender and look more like spring onions; they are not suitable for soups. Leeks and potatoes make good classic French recipes.

There are many recipes of leek and potato soups, some fancy with chicken broth, onion and cream, like the Vichyssoise, which is enjoyed cold. Because we had soup every evening, my mum made a healthier version: she just added garlic and herbs from her garden to add flavours. Leeks is a humble vegetable which is used in the classic pot-au-feu and can be made in gratin with a béchamel, or served cold as a starter with mustard dressing.

I missed potatoes too. I particularly liked baby potatoes sautéed with olive oil topped with chopped parsley and garlic that we eat in early summer.

One veggie that I could not find and still cannot find today in Hong Kong is cardoon. Cardoon is related to artichoke and originates from the Mediterranean region, but today Lyon is its homeland. Each plant weighs about 6-8 kg. Its white stalks look like chards but its leaves are long, thorny and silver-grey, and the plants cost twice as much as chards. Like endive or the yellow Chinese chives, the plant is protected from the light to keep it white. Only the stalks are eatable. Cardoon can be stir-fried but they are best au gratin with shredded Comté on top. My mum occasionally adds bone marrow, nicely called "amourettes", which also means "fleeting romance" in French, as per the Lyonnais recipe. You often find cardoons already sliced and strung at market stalls as it takes time to prepare them and their juice will blacken the hands. To help whiten the stalks, cardoons are washed with water mixed with milk. Some cooks even add milk in the cooking water. The Italians like to eat cardoons in hotpot or "hot bath[8]" but the broth is neither oil, soup stock nor melted cheese but anchovy sauce. The blanched cardoon strips are dipped in the thick sauce that is served in a pot over a candle to keep it warm. Other vegetables are also prepared for this dish to make it a complete feast.

---

[8]   The dish is called "Bagna cauda" in Italian.

Part 10

Substitutes and fusion

Both French and Chinese cuisines are delicious, refined and varied, and there are a few Chinese dishes that remind me of French dishes, for example, pork terrine served with black vinegar (Shanghainese dish) is a good substitute for headcheese. The latter consists of the whole pork head (including ear and tongue) that is cooked with vegetables and veal knuckles, then minced and made into a terrine. The gelatinous-like broth (due to the veal knuckles) is used to hold the meats together.

When I am in France, it is easy to make Chinese-style cuisine by adding ingredients like black Chinese fungus, soya sauce and oyster sauce. My (future) husband used to make chicken stew with Chinese mushrooms to impress me first at the university hall and later my parents at their home. That was one of his ways of attracting me to follow him back to live in Hong Kong! Food is truly a strong incentive to win hearts and love.

In Hong Kong, I use garlic, olive oil and aromatic herbs, such as bay leaves and thyme that I bring back from my mum's herbs garden to give a Provencal flavour to my cuisine. Summer gourds like chayote, luffa or fuzzy melon can be stewed with local tomatoes and eggplants and make a Chinese style "ratatouille". I stir-fry separately the gourds in olive oil and garlic first, and then add thyme and bay leaves in the vegetable stew.

Bok choy can be cooked the same way as Swiss chards: the white stems can be stir-fried and the green tops chopped and added in an omelette.

Baked stuffed courgettes and tomatoes are popular French summer dishes. Similarly, local gourds (bitter melon, winter melon, mouse gourd or fuzzy melon) and tomatoes can also be stuffed with minced meat, aromatic herbs, garlic and bread crumbs, and baked. Eggs can be added in the mixture to give a softer consistency to the filling. You can also add cooked rice in the mixture.

Another way to cook gourds is to make fritters. The slices of gourds are first coated in seasoned flour, secondly in beaten eggs and lastly in breadcrumbs. Italians use this method a lot. Not only they coat vegetables with breadcrumbs but also mushrooms, zucchini flowers and meat. Who has not tried the Italian style breaded veal chops?

Recently I was asked by a TV programme to cook "eggplant with minced pork and salted fish", a famous Cantonese dish. I usually cook it with anchovies instead of dried fish because my husband, like many other Chinese people, think that salted fish is not good for health, especially if you eat too much of it. I recall when I first tried a tiny piece of salted fish. Wow! It was like eating crude salt! Salted fish, like kimchi, is a nice condiment that goes well with steamed rice. My mother-in-law used to steam a slice of dried fish in her rice cooker. Like many people living in Asia's coastal areas, she enjoyed the strong flavour of the fish.

I had no idea how to buy salted fish. The salesperson of the dried goods store that I went to in Tai Po explained to me that the fish she sold were from Bangladesh and thus the tastiest and freshest that one can find. According to the pattern of the scales, she could tell if the fish had been set to dry when it was still fresh and alive. Poor animal! Placed in salt and left to dry without being gutted. But if it was the best, how could I not be convinced and buy it? I was not disappointed by the powerful flavour of the product and my environmental bag could testify it for a while!

Part 11

Idiomatic expressions related to food

There are lots of French fool-related idioms or expressions. Here are a few:

1. "Occupe-toi de tes oignons" (take care of your onions) = mind your own business.

2. "Les carottes sont cuites" (the carrots are cooked) = your goose is cooked (you are about to face the consequences).

3. "Faire le poireau" (to do the leek – imagine a leek stuck in the ground!) = to hang around.

4. "En faire tout un fromage" (make a whole cheese out of it) = make a fuss.

5. "Espèce de patate" (kind of spud) = you!

6. "Recevoir une chataîgne" (receive a chestnut) = receive a blow.

7. "Racontez des salades" (tell salads) = say lies.

8. "Ce film était un navet" (this movie was a turnip) = this movie was a dud.

9. "La cerise sur le gâteau" (the cherry on the cake) = it is a bonus (finishing touch).

10. "Avoir la cerise" (to have the cherry) = have bad "luck.

11. "Ne plus avoir un radis" (not have a radish left) = not have a penny left.

12. "Prendre quelqu'un pour une poire" (take someone for a pear) = take somebody for a mug.

13. "Etre dans les pommes cuites" (to be in cooked apples) = very tired.

14. "C'est pour ma pomme" (it's for my apple) = it's my treat (but you don't want to!)

15. "Tomber dans les pommes" (to fall in the apples) = faint.

16. "Travailler pour des prunes" (work for prunes) = work for nothing.

17. "Bouts de chou" (bits of cabbage) = small kids.

18. "Bête comme chou" (stupid as a cabbage) = dead simple.

19. "Courir sur le haricot" (run on the bean) = get on somebody's nerve.

20. "Avoir un cœur d'artichaut" (to have an artichoke heart) = fall in love easily.

21. "Avoir le melon" (to have the melon) = puffed-up with pride.

22. "Par-dessus le marché" (on top of the deal) = on top of that / into the bargain.

In Hong Kong, the importance of food is expressed through common expressions. Here are a few Cantonese colloquial food-related phrases:

1. "Let's go yum cha!": This is the equivalent of "I'll call you!" The first time I heard it, I really took it seriously and was waiting for my husband's former classmates to call us and set a date to have dim-sum together. Unless a precise date is mentioned, don't expect the other party to call you soon! In other words, "I don't plan on calling you."

2. "Have you eaten yet?": The first time I heard it was in the middle of the afternoon. I was taken aback by the cleaning lady at the place I was working at, who had asked me whether I had had my lunch or not. Did I really understand what she said? My reply was quite stupid: "of course, it is already 3:00 pm." This is a polite greeting and the best reply is "yes, what about you?"

3. Congee: Talking too long on a phone – Bou¹ din⁶-wa⁶ juk¹ (make a call / phone – congee).

4. Tofu: Verbally taking advantage of a woman (usually sexually-related): Sik⁶ dau⁶-fu⁶. To fool someone: to cheat a ghost eating tofu: Aak¹ gwai² sik⁶ dau⁶-fu⁶ or Tam³ gwai² sik⁶ dau⁶-fu⁶.

5. Lemon: be rejected: Eat lemon / Sik⁶ ning⁴-mung¹. Rejecting someone / Bei² ⁹ yan⁴ sik⁶ ning⁴-mung¹.

6. BBQ pork: Eat BBQ pork: Sik⁶ cha¹-siu¹ (= easy job).

---

⁹ Change of tone from 6 to 2.

Part 12

Markets' specificities

Markets' worth visiting

Hong Kong counts about 180 markets, of which 74 are run by the Food and Environmental Hygiene Department.

I have moved many times over the past 30 years and got to know the markets in the different districts where I lived in or where I bought at for convenience.

I like the street markets along the lanes leading down to Central district, the famous Chun Yeung Street market with the tram line running right through it in North Point, the small, dark and messy Nam Shan Estate market in Shek Kip Mei, the street markets in Nelson Street, Argyle Street and Reclamation Road in Mongkok, the indoor markets in Shatin, and finally Fu Shin market and the government-run market in Tai Po. I like exploring other places, but will do my shopping at Tai Po for the sake of convenience and also because these markets are really nice, well stocked and have a rich variety of food.

Here is a list of markets that I am familiar with or think they are worth visiting.

Street markets

Hong Kong Island:

1. Central: Graham Street market is one of the oldest
    street markets that is still operating, and is now
    a famous tourist attraction. It dates back more
    than 160 years. Many of the stalls that used to be
    on Gage Street at the junction of Graham Street
    have moved indoors due to the redevelopment
    of the area. The booths in the steep and narrow
    pedestrian lane have been replaced with standard
    metal kiosks, similar to newsagents' booths or the
    market stalls in Fa Yuen Street.

2. Wanchai: Wanchai Road used to be full of hawkers
    and stalls. Many sellers have moved to the indoor
    municipal market (a building with entrances both
    on Queen's Road East and Cross Street). Today
    Wanchai Road, Tai Wo Street and Stone Nullah Lane
    have a handful of shops (market style) extending
    their business onto the pavements.
    a. Cross Street market
    b. Bowrington Road market.

3. North Point: Chun Yeung Street Market. This is not a pedestrian street: the tram line runs right through it as well as vehicles. Shops extend their business on one side of the street. On the other side kiosks sell clothes and accessories (phone and fashion jewellery).

4. Shau Kei Wan: good for buying goat meat and fish. Really wet but conveniently located: next to MTR.

5. Causeway Bay:
   a. Goose-neck Bridge: Close to Times Square and Wanchai.
   b. Jardine's crescent has a small market at the end of the street.

Kowloon:

1. Yau-Ma-Tei:
   a. Reclamation Street
   b. Yin Chong Street (vehicles run through the street).

2. Mongkok:
   a. Nelson Road and Canton Road
   b. Argyle street (further north) to Shan Tung Street (South): stall that sells Shanghai vegetable and stem lettuce.
   c. Fa Yuen Street: fruit stall at the end of the street

3. Wong Tai Sin: Tai Shing Street. A 10-min-walk from MTR station. Indoor and outdoor.

New Territories:

1. Tai Po: Fu Shin Street. Established in 1892. Stalls on both sides of the street.

2. Sai Kung Sunday Market: some stalls sell produce from local farms.

Farmers' markets:

1. Tong Chong Street Market: operates during the winter months (from November to February).

2. Lam Tei and Tai Po, organised by the Federation of Vegetable Marketing Co-operative Societies.

3. The Organic Farmers' Market at Central

4. Organic Farmers' Market at Kadoorie Farm and Botanical Garden by Kadoorie Farm and Botanical Garden.

5. Organic Farmers' market at Mei Foo by Young Men's Christian Association.

Public covered markets

Note: number in brackets = number of stalls

Hong Kong Island:

1. Sai Wan Ho: fish (20). Stall selling halal meat.
2. Sheung Wan: fish (52); wet goods (51); meat (36); live poultry (7).
3. Bowrington Road market (closer to Causeway Bay). Stall selling halal meat.
4. Happy Valley: 2 Yuk Sau Street, called Wong Nai Chung market. Expensive.

Kowloon:

1. Yau-Ma-Tei:
   a. Kansu Street: fish (60)
   b. Wholesale fruit market
2. Kowloon City: The trendiest of all the markets.
   a. Biggest market in terms of number of food-related wet goods (193).
   b. Lots of fruit stalls (24). Fresh fruit from South-East Asia like durian, mangoes, dragon eyes, etc. Trendy place to buy very expensive fruit

       – crispy Fuji apples, perfect grapes, huge strawberries. I recall the square watermelons from Japan on sale 20 years ago.

    c. Not easy to park but lots of people from residential areas like Kowloon Tong go there. Expensive.

    d. Good area for Chiu Chow and Thai food.

    e. No air-conditioning.

3. Lok Fu: 198 Junction Road, Wang Tau Hom. Convenient as it is next to MTR station.

4. Hung Hom: fish (32); fresh meat (20)

5. Sham Shui Po:

    a. Pei Ho Street: one of the cheapest markets. The area is one of the poorest in Hong Kong.

    b. Po On Street, Cheung Sha Wan: Fruit (97); fish (26); wet goods (142).

6. Kwun Tung:

    a. Ngau Tau Kok: over 400 stalls.

    b. Po Tat market, 2 Po Lam Road in Sau Mau Ping: 43 stalls; electronic payment since October 2017.

7. Wong Tai Sin:

    a. Tai Shing Street: fruit (43)

    b. Ngau Chi Wan market: wet goods (152)

New Territories:

1. Tsuen Wan: large, clean and bright market. Wet goods: (152).

2. Yuen Long: Tai Kiu: fish (43).

3. Sai Kung[10]: fish (35).

4. Sha Tau Kok: the most remote market.

5. Tai Po: the most luxurious market.

   a. Tai Po Hui market (municipal building); opened in September 2004. About 300 stalls (including dried goods). Beautiful air-conditioned market. Fish (65): highest number of fishmongers in town; poultry (5); fresh meat (28); wet goods (59). Only a few stalls selling fruit – which are more expensive than stalls sold in the street nearby. Specialist stalls that sell ginger & garlic, dried salty fish, Chinese sausage & waxed pork belly, dumplings and pasta, roots, herbs and medicinal weeds. Organic vegetables stalls are located at the back.

   b. Tai Yuen market: Opened in 1980. Operated by Link Reit and renovated in 2011. About 50 fresh food stalls. Restaurants nearby.

---

[10] You can buy fish at the floating market from fishermen selling their catches along the piers straight from their boats.

Part 13

Gardening

Why farming

Fresh produce is the key element to make good food and healthy eating. From an early age, I have been lucky to be able to enjoy home-grown greens and understand the difficulty in growing them and thus their value. Gardening and eating fresh vegetables have played an important role in my younger life. My mum was a homemaker and, in addition to raising her three children and two of my cousins, she did everything at home: not only cleaning but also sewing, knitting, baking and gardening. Long before it was fashionable for city dwellers to rent a plot of land to grow their own vegetables and herbs, gardening was already something common in France. The outdoor activity allowed our family to have cheap (no labour cost!) and almost pesticide-free produce.

I was about 10 years old when my parents moved to a bigger house which had a piece of land at the back. However, the soil was poor and with so many stones that my parents had to spend a lot of time getting rid of them. I recall my first summer holiday after moving to our new home when my sister, brother and I were asked to pitch in the uninteresting and tiring task. We'd better not complain of being bored at home, otherwise my mum would immediately suggest picking up a few more stones. It took us a few months to clear the largest pebbles. Even though we all worked hard, we had never been able to remove them all. But despite this drawback, our vegetables, with the help of horse manure that we bought at nearby farms, grew well.

In spring we had sweet peas, snow peas, baby potatoes, radishes, Swiss chards and lettuce. In summer we had green beans, courgettes, aubergines, tomatoes and aromatic herbs. The latter are very important to perfect summer dishes; a string of parsley or some basil leaves will give a Mediterranean flavour to a simple pasta dish. In autumn we had carrots, leeks, cabbages, pumpkins and cardoons. Still we were not self-sufficient and had to buy extra and different kinds of vegetables at the market.

We also had a few rows of strawberries. I never liked them and wonder why Hong Kong people are crazy about them and willing to pay exorbitant prices to eat the red fruit. I much preferred the raspberries and redcurrants that we planted at the rear of our backyard. My mum made a delicious jelly with the latter. But my favourite fruit was and still is apricot. We also had two cherry trees. I did not realise then how lucky I was to be able to eat freshly picked fruits. Today I am often disappointed by tasteless fruit that have been picked too early in order to travel better.

My dad was a foreman in a factory making loom's mechanical parts and did not know much about gardening. It was only after he had retired that he started devoting some of his time to our vegetable garden; he was much proud of his plantations. Before, it was my maternal grandfather who came a few mornings each week to tend to our vegetable plot. A former postman, he was an expert in gardening: he knew when it was the best time for planting seeds and transplanting, and for that followed the agricultural calendar relying on the moon phases. I still recall some agriculture terms he employed and when he was telling my mum that a certain seed needed to be planted on the waning moon and another type on the new moon. He would also explain to her that he liked to hoe the dirt between the rows of green beans before the rain came so that the plants would better benefit.

After we had helped to clear stones from our garden, my mum would allot a small plot to each one of us to grow our own vegetables as a way to thank my sister, my brother and me and encourage us to become interested in gardening. My mum also had the chance to grow vegetables on her own when she was small and that is why she thought of carrying on the tradition and passed it on to her children. My son also had a short gardening experience at my parents' home. One summer my dad gave him garden radish seeds to sow. The small pink vegetables could grow in such a very short time that he was able to see the small leaves growing steadily within his 3-week summer holidays and eat the tubers before returning to Hong Kong. And guess what: his radishes were the best in the world! My son also learnt that potatoes did not grow on plants like tomatoes. I recall his surprise when my mum pulled plants out of the soil and he saw the small yellowish balls attached to the roots.

Similarly, it is common for city kids not to know how the milk is produced and to think that they either come from the fridge or the supermarket.

Children, just like adults, like to think that their home-grown vegetables taste better than those produced by professionals, to the extent that some vegetables which they usually don't like would suddenly turn delicious. For example, my sister who hated tomatoes started to like the little red fruit that she herself grew in her garden. Another interesting phenomenon was that when my brother grew Romaine lettuce, my parents who had never planted this variety before were so pleased with his produce that they decided to grow some themselves.

Like today's city dwellers who grow herbs and vegetables on building rooftops or a plot of leased land, I enjoyed very much taking care of my little garden all by myself, although it was not easy. I had to water and weed my plantation on my own, but the joy and satisfaction of eating my own produce was worth the effort. As far as my farming experience is concerned, I don't recall any extraordinary harvest or interesting crop in particular. I liked planting flowers, particularly "immortals" which, as their name implies, were long-lasting. I cut them and hung them upside down to dry and made bouquets to brighten the living room during the grey and cold winter days. I also recall planting daisies and the little flowers proliferated so well that the vegetable garden of my parents was overflowing with daisies!

It was difficult to recognise and name all the aromatic herbs that my mum liked to grow in our garden. Some of them, such as thyme, rosemary and sage, were both used in cooking and making herbal tea while verbena and mint were only used to make herbal tea. On one occasion, my sister mistook carnation leaves for rosemary. She loved to cook and always made us try new and delicious recipes, but one day my parents found the dish that she made had a peculiar taste. They could not figure out why until they asked my sister where she went to get the rosemary required in her recipe. To our surprise, we learnt that we had just tasted a carnation-flavoured sauce as she had mistakenly used carnation leaves instead of rosemary. Luckily for us, this plant was not toxic.

My parents treated potatoes with a special mixture that they sprayed on the plants when there were too many potato beetles threatening the output of their crop. Sometimes my sister, my brother and I would take a box and pick up doryphores. I can't recall what we did with the insects after collecting them. My dad also sprayed pesticide once a year to remove the tough weeds in our courtyard. The spray must have contaminated our vegetables. At that time, although we were aware of the danger of chemicals on our health, we were not overly concerned, as we were not using strong dosage and only one time. We were happy: our tomatoes were sweeter than those bought from greengrocers that were produced in large quantity, forced to grow quickly and without any defects. We were lucky to be able to enjoy comparatively healthier food than city citizens who had to buy greens.

Other farming methods

Will urban farming and growing cherry tomatoes, lettuce and herbs on rooftops become outdated when today we can eat food produced in your kitchen or dining room? Have you heard of this method that allows city dwellers to build vertical or window gardens and grow vegetables out of recycled plastic containers on window sills, shelves, unused table tops or in a corner of a floor space? Window farming uses a hydroponic system, which doesn't need soil, but clay pebbles, rock wool, planters, a good watering system and liquid nutrients; and of course seeds! Kits can be purchased, or if you are a handy person you can self-build your garden. There are different ways of building your hydroponic garden, for instance, some people use pool noodles (buoyant polyethylene foam) instead of rock wool, etc., but the concept is the same: build, grow and eat your own organic food! Can this system be the future garden of every citizen and be a solution to climate change? Liquid nutrients can be homemade with food waste and worms (vermicomposting) or stinging nettle. My parents used to macerate nettle that grew wild in our garden and made a tea with it to water seedlings. The stinging plants are rich in nitrogen, which is also a good activator for compost. I remember that the liquid smelled very bad! Later my parents made compost with vegetables, fruit peels and egg shells.

Hydroponic farming is another farming technique. It can be developed on a large scale in cities or industrial parks in farms that look like laboratories. In Hong Kong, the trend has seen these laboratories-like expanding in industrial buildings. Plants grow in water where farmers, or should I call them technicians, monitor their growth on computers. Home growers can use a dedicated application to do the same. When natural light is low, LED tubes can remedy such deficiency which will increase the greens' production. This technique presents various advantages, notably a faster growth and a higher yield than conventional farming. Furthermore, farmers can say goodbye to lumbago because plants grow on higher grounds

The technique is not without controversy and its opponents claim that vegetables growing in water are tasteless and large-scale farms are detrimental to small scale conventional farmers. In France, hydroponic farming has been gaining popularity over the past years, tomato being the main produce.

Another technique is aeroponics. The latter differs in the way that plants are suspended in the air and their roots are sprayed with nutrient-rich water solution.

I recently visited a bionic farm in the New Territories where the vegetables and aromatic herbs are fed with nutrients made with plants and weeds fermented with sugar, sprayed via an underground drip irrigation system. The plant-base nutrients allow the soil to get richer and richer over time. Music is played in the background and contributes to the plants' growth.

Aquaponic is another farming system that combines raising fish or other aquatic animals and growing plants in water. Fish excrement is used as nutrients for the plants and water is cleansed and re-circulated back to the fish pond. This technique is complex and difficult to control and fewer farms are using it. I recall visiting a farm in the New Territories in 2012, which just started experimenting with this technique at that time. Today, in Hong Kong, the number of farms practising hydroponic farming is lower than aquaponics but their yield is higher.

After moving to our new home, I had to help clearing stones from our garden during my first summer holiday.

My dad taught my son how to sow radish seeds. They grew so fast that my son was able to see the small green leaves growing steadily within his 3-week summer holidays and eat the pink tubers before returning to Hong Kong. His radishes were the best in the world!

In our own gardens, my sister grew her little red fruit, my brother his Romaine crop, and I myself liked to plant flowers. The vegetable garden was overflowing with my little blooming daisies!

Part 14

English-Cantonese Vocabulary of shopping at wet markets

All the vocabulary listed includes English, Cantonese romanisation and Chinese characters. I used the Yale romanisation for the spelling, and numbers 1-6 to indicate the tones.

Notes:

1. The tone for the same word might be different depending on the context.
2. Readers may find this on-line Cantonese pronunciation dictionary useful:

   https://humanum.arts.cuhk.edu.hk/Lexis/lexi-can/

Weights, special numbers, measure words and money / chung⁵-leung⁶, dak⁶-bit⁶ sou³-ji⁶, leung⁶-chi⁴ & chin² / 重量、特別數字、量詞 & 錢

English	Romanisation	Chinese
Weights		
1 catty	yat¹ gan¹	一斤
½ catty	bun³ gan¹	半斤
1 ½ catties	gan¹ bun³	斤半
2 ½ catties	leung⁵ gan¹ bun³	兩斤半
1 tael	yat¹ leung²	一兩
1 pound	yat¹ bong⁶	一磅
Special numbers		
2 (used for numbers; e.g. phone number, zip code, etc.)	yi⁶	二
2 (used together with nouns; e.g. 2 cabbages)	leung⁵	兩
Measure words (MW)		
1 whole piece of (e.g. cake, bell pepper)	yat¹ go³ (most common MW)	一個
1 piece of (e.g. a piece of cake)	yat¹ gin⁶	一件
1 portion of	yat¹ fan⁶	一份
1 bundle of	yat¹ jaat³	一紮
1 dozen of	yat¹ da¹	一打

1 irregular piece of (e.g. ginger)	yat^1 gau^6	一嚿
1 flat piece of (e.g. pork chop)	yat^1 faai^3	一塊
1 long piece of (e.g. fish, radish)	yat^1 tiu^4	一條
1 head (e.g. chicken)	yat^1 jek^3	一隻
1 bottle of	yat^1 jeun^1	一樽
1 brick of (e.g. tofu)	yat^1 jyun^1	一磚
1 grain / granule of (e.g. red bean)	yat^1 lap^1	一粒
1 slice of	yat^1 pin^3	一片
1 box of	yat^1 hap^6	一盒
1 bag of	yat^1 baau^1	一包
Money		
HK$1	Spoken: yat^1 man^1 Written: yat^1 yun^4	一蚊 一元
HK$1.50 HK$0.50	go^3 bun^3 ng^5 hou^4-ji^2	個半 五毫子
How much?	gei^2 chin^2?	幾錢？

At the meat stalls / yuk^6-dong^3 / 肉檔

Pork / jyu1-yuk6 / 豬肉

1. Lean pork / sau^3-yuk^6 / 瘦肉
2. Pork brisket belly / jyu^1-naam^5-yuk^6 / 豬腩肉
3. Pork belly / ng^5-fa^1-naam^5 / 五花腩
4. Pork fillet / jyu^1-lau^5 / 豬柳
5. Pork chop / jyu^1-pa^2 / 豬扒
6. Pork shank / jyu^1-jin^2 / 豬展 (jin^2 / 展 is a borrowed character)
7. Pork neck / jyu^1-geng^2-yuk^6 / 豬頸肉
8. Pork cheek / jyu^1-min^6-yuk^6 / 豬面肉 . Some people call it min^6-jyu^1-dan^1 / 面珠墩 .
9. Pork collar butt / mui^4-tau^2 / 梅頭
10. Tenderloin (US) or pork fillet (British) / lau^5-mui^2 / 柳梅
11. Pork bones / jyu^1-gwat^1 / 豬骨
12. Shoulder blade (meat and bone; excellent for soups) / sai^1-si^1-gwat^1 / 西施骨 . Sai^1-si^1 / 西施 is one of the famous four renowned Four Beauties of ancient China.
13. Pork cartilage / jyu^1-yun^5-gwat^1 / 豬軟骨
14. Pork ribs / paai^4-gwat^1 / 排骨

15. Spareribs / naam⁵-paai² / 腩排 (nicer than paai⁴-gwat¹ / 排骨；fei¹-paai² / 飛排 is even better)
16. Pork hock / yun⁴-tai⁴ / 元蹄
17. Pork trotters (fore limbs) / jyu¹-sau² / 豬手
18. Pork trotters (rear limbs) / jyu¹-geuk³ / 豬腳
19. Pork tongue / jyu¹-lei⁶ / 豬脷
20. Pork tail / jyu¹-mei⁵ / 豬尾
21. Pork ears / jyu¹-yi⁵ / 豬耳
22. Pork snout / jyu¹-bei⁶ / 豬鼻
23. Pork liver / jyu¹-yeun² / 豬膶
24. Pork intestines / jyu¹-daai⁶-cheung² / 豬大腸
25. Pork spleen / jyu¹-waang⁴-lei⁶ / 豬橫脷
26. Pork lungs / jyu¹-fai³ / 豬肺

Beef / ngau⁴-yuk⁶ / 牛肉

1. Beef brisket / ngau⁴-naam⁵ / 牛腩
2. Beef fillet / ngau⁴-lau⁵ / 牛柳
3. Beef steak / ngau⁴-pa² / 牛扒
4. Beef tendon / ngau⁴-gan¹ / 牛筋
5. Beef shank meat / ngau⁴-jin² / 牛展

Poultry / ga¹-kam⁴ / 家禽

1. Chicken meat / gai¹-yuk⁶ / 雞肉
2. Chicken fillet / gai¹-pa² / 雞扒
3. Chicken breast / gai¹-hung¹ / 雞胸
4. Chicken thigh or drumstick / gai¹-bei² / 雞髀
5. Chicken wing / gai¹-yik⁶ / 雞翼
6. Chicken feet (cuisine) / gai¹-geuk³ / 雞腳
7. Deep-fried chicken feet / fung⁶-jaau² / 鳳爪

Other vocabulary / kei⁴-ta¹ chi⁴-wui⁶ / 其他詞彙
Special requests:

1. Minced / gaau²-seui³ or min⁵-ji⁶ / 攪碎 or 免治 (transliteration)
2. Sliced / chit³ pin² / 切片
3. To chop (ribs) / jaam² / 斬
4. Bigger pieces / daai⁶-gau⁶ di¹ / 大嚿啲
5. Smaller pieces / sai³-gau⁶ di¹ / 細嚿啲
6. More fat on the meat / fei⁴ di¹ / 肥啲
7. Less fat on the meat / sau³ di¹ / 瘦啲

8. A little bit fat / siu²-siu² fei⁴ / 少少肥
9. How to cook? / dim² jyu²? / 點煮？
   a. For stewing / man¹ ge³ / 炆嘅
   b. For stir-frying / chaau² ge³ / 炒嘅
   c. For steaming / jing¹ ge³ / 蒸嘅
   d. For soup / bou¹-tong¹ ge³ / 煲湯嘅 (quick soup: gwan²-tong¹ ge³ / 滾湯嘅)
   e. For hot pot / da²-bin¹-lou⁴ ge³ / 打邊爐嘅 (fo²-wo¹ yung⁶ ge³ / 火煱 or 火鍋用嘅)
10. Miscellaneous:
    a. Sold out / maai⁶-saai³ / 賣曬

At the fish stalls / yu⁴-dong³ / 魚檔

Seafood / hoi²-chaan² / 海產

1. Mussel / cheng¹-hau² / 青口
2. Razor clam / sing-ji² / 蟶子
3. Clam / hin² / 蜆
4. Whelk or sea snail / lo² / 螺
5. Scallop / daai³-ji² / 帶子
6. Oyster / hou⁴ / 蠔
7. Octopus / baat³-jaau²-yu⁴ / 八爪魚
8. Squid / yau⁴-yu² / 魷魚
9. Cuttlefish / mak⁶-yu⁴ / 墨魚 (墨 means "ink")
10. Abalone/ baau¹-yu⁴ / 鮑魚
11. Shrimp / ha¹ / 蝦
12. Prawn / daai⁶-ha¹ / 大蝦
13. Lobster / lung⁴-ha¹ / 龍蝦
14. Crab / haai⁵ / 蟹
15. Shanghai hairy crab / daai⁶-jaap⁶-haai⁵ / 大閘蟹

Saltwater fish / haam⁴-seui²-yu² / 鹹水魚

1. Pomfret / chong¹-yu² / 鯧魚
2. Giant grouper / lung⁴-dan² / 龍躉
3. Grouper / sek⁶-baan¹ / 石斑
4. Salmon / saam¹-man⁴-yu² / 三文魚
5. Sole / lung⁴-lei⁶ / 龍利 or 龍脷
6. Skate fish / pou⁴-yu⁴ or pou¹-yu⁴ / 鯆魚
7. Devil fish / mo¹-gwai²-yu² / 魔鬼魚

8. Mackerel / gaau^1-yu^2 / 鮫魚
9. Four finger threadfin / ma^5-yau^5-yu^2 / 馬友魚
10. Golden threadfin bream / hung^4-saam^1-yu^2 / 紅衫魚
11. Grey mullet / wu^1-tau^2 / 烏頭
12. Yellow croaker / wong^4-fa^1-yu^2 / 黃花魚
13. Amberjack or yellow tail / si^1-yu^2 / 鰤魚
14. Sea bass or perch / lou^4-yu^2 / 鱸魚
15. Mangrove red snapper / hung^4-yau^2 / 紅友
16. Two-spot red snapper / hung^4-chou^4 / 紅鰽
17. Silver cod / ngan^4-syut^3-yu^2 / 銀鱈魚
18. Marbled rockfish / sek^6-sung^4-yu^2 / 石崇魚 (for soups)

Freshwater fish / taam^5-sui^2-yu^2 / 淡水魚

1. Grass carp / waan^5-yu^2 / 鯇魚
2. Bighead or black silver carp / daai^6-yu^2 / 大 魚 . Some people only buy the head as it is the tastiest part of the fish.
3. Dace or mud carp / leng^4-yu^2 / 鯪魚 . Lots of bones. Good for mincing.
4. Common carp / lei^5-yu^2 / 鯉魚
5. Mandarin fish / gwai^3-fa^1-yu^2 / 桂花魚 . Its nickname is fresh water grouper / taam^5-seui^2 sek^6-baan^1 / 淡水石斑 as it is comparable to the saltwater grouper species.
6. Japanese eel / baak^6-sin^5 / 白鱔 . Chinese restaurants serve it sliced and steamed with black bean and garlic. At Japanese restaurants, it is called maan^6-yu^4 / 鰻魚 .
7. Asian swamp eel / wong^4-sin^5 / 黃鱔

Other vocabulary / kei^4-ta^1 chi^4-wui^6 / 其他詞彙

1. Fish / yu^2 or yu^4 / 魚
2. Seafood / hoi^2-sin^1 / 海鮮
3. Sea products / hoi^2-chaan^2 / 海產
4. Shellfish / bui^3-leui^6 / 貝類
5. Fish scales / yu^4-leun^4 / 魚鱗
6. Minced mud carp / leng^4-yu^4-yuk^6 / 鯪魚肉
7. Fish fillet / yu^4-lau^5 / 魚柳
8. Sliced fresh fish / yu^4-pin^2 / 魚片
9. To pan-fry a fish / jin^1 yu^2 / 煎魚
10. To steam a fish / jing^1 yu^2 / 蒸魚

At the grocers' / jaap⁶-fo³ pou² / 雜貨舖

Dried goods / gon¹-fo³ / 乾貨

1. Chinese figs / mou⁴-fa¹-gwo² / 無花果
2. Brown or honey dates / mat⁶-jou² / 蜜棗
3. Jujubes or Chinese red dates / hung⁴-jou² / 紅棗
4. Apricot kernels / naam⁴-bak¹-hang⁶ / 南北杏
5. Lotus seeds / lin⁴-ji² / 蓮子
6. Chinese yam / waai⁴-saan¹ / 淮山
7. Gingko nuts / baak⁶-gwo² / 白果
8. Fox nuts or Makhana / chi⁴-sat⁶ / 茨實
9. Chinese pearl barley or Job's tears / yi³-mai⁵ / 薏米
10. Adzuki beans or rice beans / chek³-siu²-dau⁶ / 赤小豆
11. Red beans / hung⁴-dau² / 紅豆
12. Mung beans / luk⁶-dau² / 綠豆
13. Black-eyed peas / mei⁴-dau² / 眉豆
14. Goji berries / gei²-ji² / 杞子
15. Black Chinese fungus or cloud ear fungus / wan⁴-yi⁵ / 雲耳
16. Chinese mushroom or dried shiitake / dung¹-gu¹ / 冬菇
17. Dried shrimps / ha¹-mai⁵ / 蝦米

Seasoning & Condiments / tiu⁴-mei⁶-liu² & pui³-liu² / 調味料 & 配料

1. Fermented red bean curd / naam⁴-yu⁵ / 南乳
2. Fermented white bean curd / fu⁶-yu⁵ / 腐乳
3. Hoisin sauce / hoi²-sin¹ jeung³ / 海鮮醬
4. Soy sauce / saang¹-chau¹ or si⁶-yau⁴ / 生抽 or 豉油
5. Dark soy sauce / lou⁵-chau¹ / 老抽
6. Oyster sauce / hou⁴-yau⁴ / 蠔油
7. Sesame oil / ma⁴-yau⁴ / 麻油
8. Fermented black bean / dau⁶-si⁶ / 豆豉
9. XO sauce / XO jeung³ / XO 醬
10. Preserved duck egg or thousand-year-old egg / pei⁴-daan² / 皮蛋
11. Salted duck egg / haam⁴-daan² / 鹹蛋
12. Pickled mustard tuber / ja³-choi³ / 榨菜
13. Mung bean vermicelli / fan²-si¹ / 粉絲

At the stall selling soy derived products
/ dau⁶-fu⁶ dong³ / 豆腐檔

Soy products / dau²-leui⁶ sik⁶-ban² / 豆類食品

1. Bean curd sheets / fu⁶-juk¹ / 腐竹
2. Soybean sticks / ji¹-juk¹ / 枝竹
3. Deep-fried bean curd / dau⁶-fu⁶-bok¹ / 豆腐卜
4. Dry or pressed bean curd / dau⁶-fu⁶-gon¹ / 豆腐乾
5. Hard bean curd / ngaang⁶ dau⁶-fu⁶ / 硬豆腐
6. Soft bean curd / yun⁵ dau⁶-fu⁶ / 軟豆腐
7. Mung bean sprouts / nga⁴-choi³-jai² or sai³-dau² nga⁴-choi³ / 芽菜仔 or 細豆芽菜
8. Soybean sprouts / daai⁶-dau² nga⁴-choi³ / 大豆芽菜

Gluten products / fu¹-leui⁶ sik⁶-ban² / 麪類食品

1. Deep-fried gluten ball / saang¹-gan¹ / 生根
2. Gluten (gluten meat) / min⁶-gan¹ / 麵筋

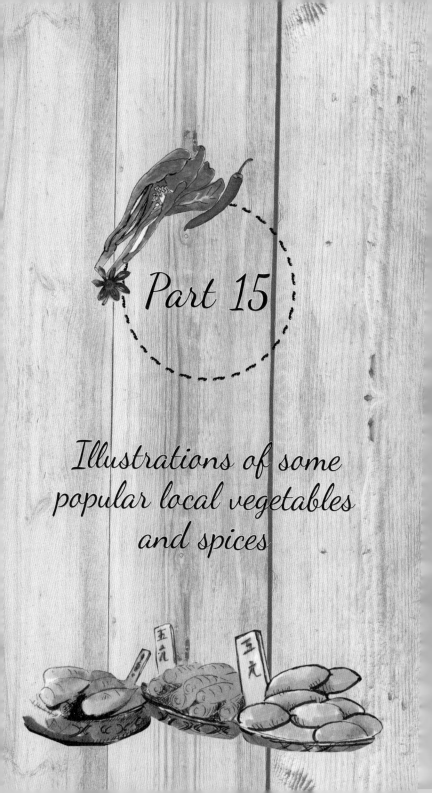

Part 15

Illustrations of some popular local vegetables and spices

Leafy vegetables

1.   Chinese flowering cabbage / choi³-sam¹ / 菜心

2.   Chinese broccoli or Chinese kale / gaai³-laan² / 芥蘭

3.   Bok choy or Chinese white cabbage / baak⁶-choi³ / 白菜

4.   Shanghai white cabbage or sow cabbage / siu²-tong⁴-choi³ / 小棠菜

5.   Tientsin cabbage or long cabbage / siu⁶-choi³ or wong⁴-nga⁴-baak⁶ / 紹菜 or 黃芽白

6.   Pea shoots / dau⁶-miu⁴ / 豆苗

7.   Spinach / bo¹-choi³ / 菠菜

8.   Amaranth or Chinese spinach / yin⁶-choi³ / 莧菜

9.   Water spinach or morning glory / ung³-choi³ or tung¹-choi³ / 蕹菜 or 通菜

10. Ceylon spinach or slippery vegetable / saan⁴-choi³ / 潺菜

11. Mustard green (and other types of mustard cabbage) / gaai³-choi³ / 芥菜

12. Mustard cabbage head / baau¹-gaai³-choi³ / 包芥菜

13. Celery / sai¹-kan² / 西芹

14. Chinese celery / kan⁴-choi³ or tong⁴-kan² / 芹菜 or 唐芹

15. Chinese lettuce / tong⁴ saang¹-choi³ / 唐生菜

16. Indian lettuce or A-choy / yau⁴-mak⁶-choi³ / 油麥菜

17. Garland chrysanthemum / tong⁴-hou¹ / 茼蒿

18. Chinese box thorn or wolfberry / gau²-gei²-choi³ / 枸杞菜

Roots and rhizomes

1. Carrot / hung⁴-lo⁴-baak⁶ / 紅蘿蔔

2. Oriental radish / (baak⁶) lo⁴-baak⁶ / （白）蘿蔔

3. Green oriental radish / cheng¹-lo⁴-baak⁶ / 青蘿蔔

4. Sweet potato / faan¹-syu² / 蕃薯

5. Taro / wu⁶-tau² / 芋頭

6. Lotus root / lin⁴-ngau⁵ / 蓮藕

7. Kohlrabi / gaai³-laan²-tau⁴ / 芥蘭頭

8. Yam bean / sa¹-got³ / 沙葛

9. Kudzu / fan²-got³ / 粉葛

10. Bamboo shoot / juk¹-seun² / 竹筍

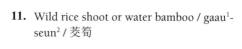

11. Wild rice shoot or water bamboo / gaau¹-seun² / 茭筍

12. Ginger / geung¹ / 薑

13. Arrowhead root / chi⁴-gu¹ / 慈姑 or 茨菇

Gourds

1. Winter melon / dung¹-gwa¹ / 冬瓜

2. Fuzzy melon or hairy melon / jit³-gwa¹ / 節瓜

3. Cucumber / cheng¹-gwa¹ / 青瓜

4. Eggplant / ai²-gwa¹ / 矮瓜 . Its dish name is ke²-ji² / 茄子

5. Angled luffa or silk gourd / si¹-gwa¹ or sing³-gwa¹ / 絲瓜 or 勝瓜

6. Chayote or Buddha's hand melon / fat⁶-sau²-gwa¹ / 佛手瓜

7. Yellow cucumber (old cucumber) / lou⁵-wong⁴-gwa¹ / 老黃瓜

8. Bitter melon / fu²-gwa¹ or leung⁴-gwa¹ / 苦瓜 or 涼瓜

9. Bottle gourd / wu⁴-lou⁴-gwa¹ / 胡蘆瓜

10. Sweet or bell pepper / tim⁴-jiu¹ or dang¹-lung⁴-jiu¹ / 甜椒 or 燈籠椒. If green, it is called cheng¹-tim⁴-jiu¹ / 青甜椒 or luk⁶-sik¹ dang¹-lung⁴-jiu¹ / or 綠色燈籠椒

11. Green (pointed) pepper / cheng¹-(jim¹)-jiu¹ / 青（尖）椒 (slightly spicy)

Bean, mushrooms and others

1. Yard-long beans or long beans / dau⁶-gok³ / 豆角

2. Straw mushroom / chou²-gu¹ 草菇

3. Water caltrop / ling⁴-gok³ / 菱角

4. Chinese water chestnut / ma⁵-tai² / 馬蹄

5. Stem lettuce / wo¹-seun² / 萵筍

6. Chinese chives and flowering chives / gau²-choi³ 韭菜 and gau²-choi³-fa¹ / 韭菜花

Herbs & Spices

1. Coriander / yim⁴-sai¹ / 芫茜

2. Spring onion / chung¹ / 蔥

3. Blanched Chinese chives / gau²-wong⁴ / 韭黃

4. Chinese star anise / baat³-gok³ / 八角

5. Garlic / syun³-tau⁴ / 蒜頭

6. Chilli pepper / laat⁶-jiu¹ / 辣椒

7. Parsley / faan¹-sai¹ / 蕃茜

Conclusion

Although a few things have changed over the years at markets in both Hong Kong and France, overall these places have kept their own traditional style.

Hygiene and environmental issues regarding French markets have grown over the past 30 years. Sellers of fresh products have to adapt to French regulations and have been required to store and display their goods in refrigerated vans. The use of plastic bags is today strictly regulated and digital scales are everywhere. There are also more cooked food stalls at French markets to cater for the need of the new generation who leads a busier life and appreciates convenience. Another trend is the appearance of stalls selling organic vegetables. One main difference is that live animals are prohibited and you can no longer buy live poultry at the market. Despite these changes, French markets remain an attractive weekly social event, similar to a fair that should not be missed. People feel good to buy at the market and support local farmers. Sellers come and go and the life of market-goers is marked by the weekly event.

In Hong Kong, some markets have moved indoors with the aim of making these places more hygienic and comfortable, some being fitted with air-conditioning system. Despite this apparent modernisation, some sellers, particularly greengrocers, still use mechanical balances. Large shop-like stalls that sell goods at very low prices are today more common. Like in France, organic food has also gained in popularity and you can find a few organic stalls at big markets. Throughout all these years, one of the changes is that stalls resume business sooner during the Chinese New Year than they used to.

On the other hand, Hong Kong markets are still as lively and active as before. Although there are more hygiene controls than before, the laws are not as stringent as in France, and market stalls look the same to me as they were back in 1985, except for the poultry section. However, we can still buy live chickens in the market. Plastic bags are still given to customers without any restriction.

While wet markets have kept their traditional forms, Hong Kong supermarkets have become westernised and sell fresh meat and fish.

In terms of choice of produce, today we can find Asian food at many local supermarkets in France that used to be sold only in Chinatowns. Thus, a young girl who comes to Hong Kong today will not be as surprised at the view of some veggies as I was in 1985 when I first visited a Chinese market. Vice versa, the variety of French food and French restaurants in Hong Kong has increased during the past 30 years as a result of globalisation. Nowadays, we can find more and more fusion-style restaurants in addition to Western or Chinese. We can also easily buy French mustard, cheese, baguette and wine in Hong Kong. Similarly, soya sauce, oyster sauce, bok choy, etc. are commonly found in France and many French people like to cook Chinese food from time to time and enjoy eating Chinese food at Asian restaurants.

Furthermore, enhanced production has also helped to make some food banal and accessible all over the world. For example, lamb in France or chicken in Hong Kong that used to be enjoyed only at Easter or Chinese festivals respectively are now part of our diet. Talking of diet, organic food is commonly found albeit at a higher cost and new farming techniques allow the growing of greens that are said to be healthier and better for the environment. Will these methods be widely developed in the future without jeopardising traditional farms and at a cost that is affordable for everyone?

I have learnt a lot by going to the market. Not only have I learnt the food names and how to buy, I also enjoy talking to the sellers and asking them to teach me how to cook. Eating is part of the culture. One cannot appreciate the local culture without knowing the local cuisine. I should also not forget the opportunity it gave, and still gives me, to practise speaking Cantonese and I thank all the sellers who have helped me all along my learning journey.

I hope my readers have fun reading my book and will discover some elements of Hong Kong and French markets through my personal stories. Both French and Chinese cultures are rich in tradition, with food being one essential part of the daily life. Fortunately, these traditions have not changed much during all these years.

To conclude, I wish my readers to be able to enjoy good food and have fun every day.

Acknowledgements

I thank Marie-José Pugnet who, together with her husband, has been selling at French markets for over 30 years for having kindly answered my queries and provided me with useful information.

I thank my mother for helping me revisit my childhood memories and for passing down French cultural values and traditions.

I also wish to thank all the sellers as well as my friends and family here in Hong Kong who helped me discover the Chinese markets and Chinese food.

I am grateful to the Hong Kong market sellers from whom I am buying regularly for their time and patience in answering my numerous questions.

My thanks also go to my former Mandarin teacher, Ms Xiaosha Tang, who skilfully translated this book into Chinese, my former Cantonese teacher, Ms Tammy Wong who revised the romanisation, Ms Doreen Cheng and Mrs Catherine Ghaffari who helped me in the preparation of the manuscript, and Ms

Leona Fung for her suggestions and encouragement during the realisation of the illustrations.

Last but not least, my deepest thanks go to my husband for his continuous support over the years and encouragement to learn and understand the Chinese culture and appreciate Chinese food. Without him, this book could not have been possible.